With an engaging and entertaining presentati
Method offers managers and leaders practical and insightful solutions to addressing even the most challenging dysfunctional workplace behaviors. Her approach has proved to be applicable to almost any workplace challenge and, thus far, has produced significant improvements in the workplace culture and the confidence of the leaders to manage dysfunctional behavior.

—**Jason Giesbrecht**, Executive Director,
Primary & Community Care Transformation

People come away from Marli's sessions feeling empowered, enlightened, invigorated, and positive. They have a clearer understanding of their responsibilities and greater confidence and competence in their ability to carry them out.

—**Barbara J. (Barb) Severyn**, Executive Director,
Human Resources, Camosun College

Marli's insightful, practical approach to assess dysfunction and bring the right tools and recommendations to address it has allowed the organization to take action to both resolve specific situations and to provide organizational learnings by identifying systemic issues and barriers.

—**Patricia J. Devlin**, Human Resources Officer

I always say if you are not ready to act do not engage Marli. She brings a true mirror to our leadership as a manager, director or CEO. What you see in the mirror is who you are in how you lead yourself and/or others. Marli is the best Mirror every leader needs throughout their leadership journey.

—**Francis Garwe**, B.SC., MAOM-HCM, CCM, CMP,
Director, Clinical Services, Community Health

At a time when employers face increasing scrutiny for how they address inappropriate conduct, Marli's proactive approach is a welcome salve for the issues that create the modern toxic workplace. The MIRROR Method is a model for how leaders can do the difficult work of creating kindness in the workplace and ensuring that all employees are treated fairly and respectfully.

—**Peter Eastwood**, Lawyer

The MIRROR METHOD WORKBOOK

The workplace leader's guide to ending dysfunction

MARLI RUSEN

Brilliant Idea Books

The MIRROR METHOD Workbook
ISBN: 978-1-989141-00-7

Editor: Leanne Tremblay, Mintedleaf Story Studio

Cover and Interior Design: WeMakeBooks.ca

Electronic Page Composition: WeMakeBooks.ca

Figure Designer: Darren Warner for Ideation + Persuasion

Printed and bound in Canada

CONTENTS

WELCOME!

Workplace dysfunction.

Ugh…

Whenever a manager, worker, or customer creates drama and conflict at work, the entire team feels it. Some people quit, others get sick, productivity drops, mistakes happen, and lawsuits are filed. Costs begin to climb.

You know you need to do something—these issues don't magically disappear, after all. But what can be done? And how?

This is where The MIRROR Method Workbook comes in.

If you're familiar with the book, *The MIRROR Method: How to build productive teams by ending workplace dysfunction*, you learned about a framework for detecting, diagnosing and remedying workplace dysfunction in a fair and defensible manner. (If you're not, we encourage you to read it in conjunction with this workbook or at any time that best serves you!)

This workbook gives you immediate hands-on tools and guidance for applying the MIRROR Method to real life. It's designed to help **leaders, staff, human resource (HR) professionals,** and **union representatives** in any industry.

The MIRROR Method provides the plan and the MIRROR Method Workbook shows you how to put that plan into action.

To make things easier, blank forms and checklists are included at the end of the workbook for you to customize and use.

What is The MIRROR Method?

We encourage you to use the term *mirror* as a reminder that you need to reflect on any apparent situation before you react to it.

The MIRROR Method teaches you how to:

- **Reflect on your own actions:** Everyone needs to accept responsibility for their own performance, communication, and behavior, both in relation to the dysfunction itself and in how it has been addressed.

- **Ask how your own actions may have contributed to the situation:** When we make assumptions, pre-judge or react hastily to concerns without gathering all the facts, we contribute to the problem instead of resolving it.
- **Reflect on the actions of others:** Often, individuals have no idea that their behavior is considered offensive or disruptive to the work environment. They're not aware of the negative impact they have on others. We can only expect people to change if they know their behavior or performance is an issue. In most situations, the only way to ensure this happens is by telling them. This communication is a responsibility shared by coworkers and leaders alike.
- **Reflect on systemic trends in the organization:** Senior leaders need to review and reflect on how their teams are currently functioning compared to previous years and to other teams. Leaders should routinely gather and review objective metrics on productivity, profitability, customer satisfaction, absenteeism, and turnover to reflect on whether further steps need to be taken.

Six Steps of the MIRROR Method

The MIRROR Method shows you how to accurately detect potential dysfunction in individuals and teams. It also guides you on how to objectively and defensibly evaluate apparent, potential or reported dysfunction. Finally, it helps you design a remedy for workplace dysfunction that is measured and balanced.

The six steps of the MIRROR Method are:

M – MONITOR the workplace for potential signs and symptoms of dysfunction

I – INQUIRE into the nature and extent of the potential dysfunction, using the MIRROR Triage Process, to determine the type of workplace Review to conduct

R – REVIEW the alleged dysfunction objectively, using an informal or formal process (based on the results of the Triage Process)

R – REMEDY the individual dysfunction in accordance with the results of the objective Review, using a combination of accountability and support

O – OPERATIONALLY RESTORE trust, communication and credibility among the team as a whole

R – REVISIT the scene of the dysfunction to determine whether the remedial and restorative processes were successful

General Principles

Workplace decisions rarely go unchallenged particularly where they involve allegations of inappropriate workplace behavior. However, by following a few general principles, you'll be able to respectfully defend the steps you've taken to resolve your workplace problems.

- **Consistency**: For the MIRROR Method to be defensible, it must be applied consistently. Cherry-picking allegations, based on the person involved or concern raised, causes leaders to lose credibility and undermines the success of the MIRROR Method.
- **Documentation:** When workplace decisions are challenged, leaders are asked to outline the steps they took in making their decisions and explain any delays in arriving at those decisions (in other words, "What took you so long?"). For both reasons, real-time documentation of your decision-making process is critical to your success. A Timeline of Events, such as the one outlined in Figure 1, will help you track this information in a clear and concise manner. To tell the full story behind the decision, you should include the date and type of intervention (such as interviews and meetings), any canceled meetings (by the employee or leader), the reasons for cancellations, any requests for documentation (such as medical information or certification of course completions), any delays in receiving documentation and the reported reasons for such delays.
- **It's how you do it:** The fact that an individual may be performing or behaving poorly will not be a defense for others—coworkers or leaders—treating that person with disrespect. No response, with or without The MIRROR Method, will be defensible if it is conveyed in a disrespectful or inconsiderate manner. Stonewalling, withholding information, gossiping, yelling, shunning, shaming, humiliating or belittling individuals involved in investigations, performance management or progressive discipline has no place in the modern workplace. Leaders who fail to respectfully implement the principles in the MIRROR Method expose themselves and their teams to complaints of harassment and bullying.
- **Not without question:** HR professionals or senior leaders who are tasked with supporting frontline supervisors and managers through the MIRROR Method should not equate support with blind and unconditional advocacy, particularly in the face of concerns or allegations about the specific leader involved. Allegations against leaders, at any level, need to be objectively assessed and addressed using the MIRROR Method.
- **Overcoming long-standing dysfunction:** Holding individuals accountable is never easy especially if the behavior has been tolerated. If individuals have been permitted to behave improperly or perform poorly over a prolonged period, they will be surprised to learn that this is unacceptable and needs to change. They might

Timeline of Events

Employee Name:

Date	Event (meeting, communication with employee, cancellations, coaching)	Follow-up / Action Completed

Figure 1: Timeline of Events

become hostile and defensive. They may engage in personalized attacks against others, either coworkers who come forward with concerns or workplace leaders who are holding them accountable for the first time. The most effective way to address such behavior is to use the MIRROR Method. Antagonistic behavior and insubordination in the face of workplace investigations or discipline need to be investigated separately and then remedied as stand-alone forms of dysfunction.

- **Customize the investigative team:** In situations involving minor events that have arisen recently, it is often sufficient for supervisors and managers to use the MIRROR Method to Review and resolve the situation. However, in situations involving complicated or long-standing behavioral or performance issues, it is important for others, such as senior leaders, HR, and union representatives to become involved.
- **Who and when:** Not every leader has to be involved in every step of the MIRROR Method. Frontline leaders (such as unionized forepersons, supervisors and team leaders) are often involved in "M" – Monitoring. Frontline leaders, managers and HR are involved in "I" – Inquiry and the Triage Process. In relation to "R" – Reviews, frontline leaders may conduct informal Reviews while managers, HR or external contractors conduct formal ones. The "R" – Remedies are implemented by operational leaders, with input from HR and others. External consultants likely facilitate "O" – Operational Restoration. Finally, frontline leaders, managers and HR are responsible for the final "R" – Revisiting the scene of the original dysfunction to assess whether it has been adequately addressed.
- **Roles and responsibilities**: Organizations are deemed to be aware of workplace dysfunction as soon as any leader, at any level, becomes aware of it. Accordingly, leaders at all levels need to be given clear expectations regarding their roles and responsibilities in reporting and addressing workplace dysfunction. This avoids indefensible delays and inaction caused by miscommunication within the leadership team in the course of implementing the MIRROR Method (in other words "I didn't realize I had to tell you" or "I thought you already knew" or "I thought you were doing it").
- **Accountability**: Each supervisor and leader on the team should be made aware of and held accountable for the parts of the MIRROR Method for which they will be responsible. Similarly, each department should be clear on its respective jurisdiction and responsibilities in relation to the various steps of this process.

CASE STUDY – JOE'S HARASSMENT CLAIM AGAINST DOLLARBILLS INC.

Throughout the workbook, we'll follow the story of Joe, a payroll assistant who recently began work for financial services company, DollarBills Inc.

Using the MIRROR Method, we'll show you how a workplace incident and Joe's harassment claim are handled through each step in the process.

But first, our cast of characters:

- **Joe**: a 25-year old successful college grad without much practical work experience
- **Mike**: a senior accounting team member who's been with the company for eight years
- **Laurie**: a mid-level accounting supervisor, and Joe and Mike's boss
- **You**: a senior HR manager brought in to deal with Joe's complaint

At the company, Joe joins a team that has been working together for several years. Many of them are older than Joe and spend a lot of time with each other outside of work. His boss, Laurie, is also part of this group.

Soon after starting his job, Joe has concerns about how the team operates. Based on what he learned in college, he feels the team doesn't follow standard regulatory or reporting practices. Each person seems to do their own thing.

When Joe asks Mike, the senior guy on the team, about this, Mike says: **"Listen, Junior, you're not in college anymore. This is the real world. Just relax, watch and learn."**

Joe meets with Laurie to talk about his concerns and Mike's response. Laurie tells him to be more open and flexible.

Joe feels dismissed by the team and posts about his experience on Facebook.

Someone sees the post and sends it to Laurie.

When Joe arrives at work the next day, he notices that no one is talking to him, and he's given menial tasks to do alone.

Joe leaves work shortly after this without notifying anyone.

Later that day, you (HR) receive a voice mail message from Joe indicating that he is off work due to harassment.

STEP 1 — MONITORING THE WORKPLACE

M
Monitoring

Let's get started!

First, it's important to remember that no team is ever dysfunction-free. Even successful teams experience dysfunction at some point. The health of a team lies in detecting and resolving the dysfunction as soon as it appears.

That's why Step 1, Monitoring the Workplace, is critical. In this step, you're expected to routinely and proactively Monitor the following factors:

- Behavior and performance of individuals
- Communication and interpersonal dynamics between individuals (coworkers and leaders) on the same or different teams
- Overall climate, productivity and health of the team to determine if there is dysfunction that needs to be resolved

Once issues, or DOTs of dysfunction, are detected, the other steps of the MIRROR Method are triggered.

What Are DOTs of Dysfunction?

Before we go much further, let's define *workplace dysfunction.*

In Figure 2, Role of the Individual or Team in Workplace Dysfunction, a functional team is represented by the circle of individuals who work together to achieve specific deliverables. The arrows represent common ways in which this functionality is compromised, resulting in a failure to meet necessary objectives by established deadlines.

As a leader, you are expected to provide clear communication to your staff on the exact nature of their individual and collective expectations at work. Each team member is expected to show up and perform their work in an accurate and timely manner; and to treat everyone at work with basic civility and respect while doing so.

Workplace dysfunction occurs when "something happens" and as a result, the team's functional bubble gets pierced (this is the interference noted above). The piercing is a DOT of dysfunction (DOT stands for **D**ysfunction **O**n **T**eam). The dysfunction results in reduced functioning ("dys-function") in an individual or team at a given time. It is not a

M
Monitoring

Role of the Individual or Team in Workplace Dysfunction

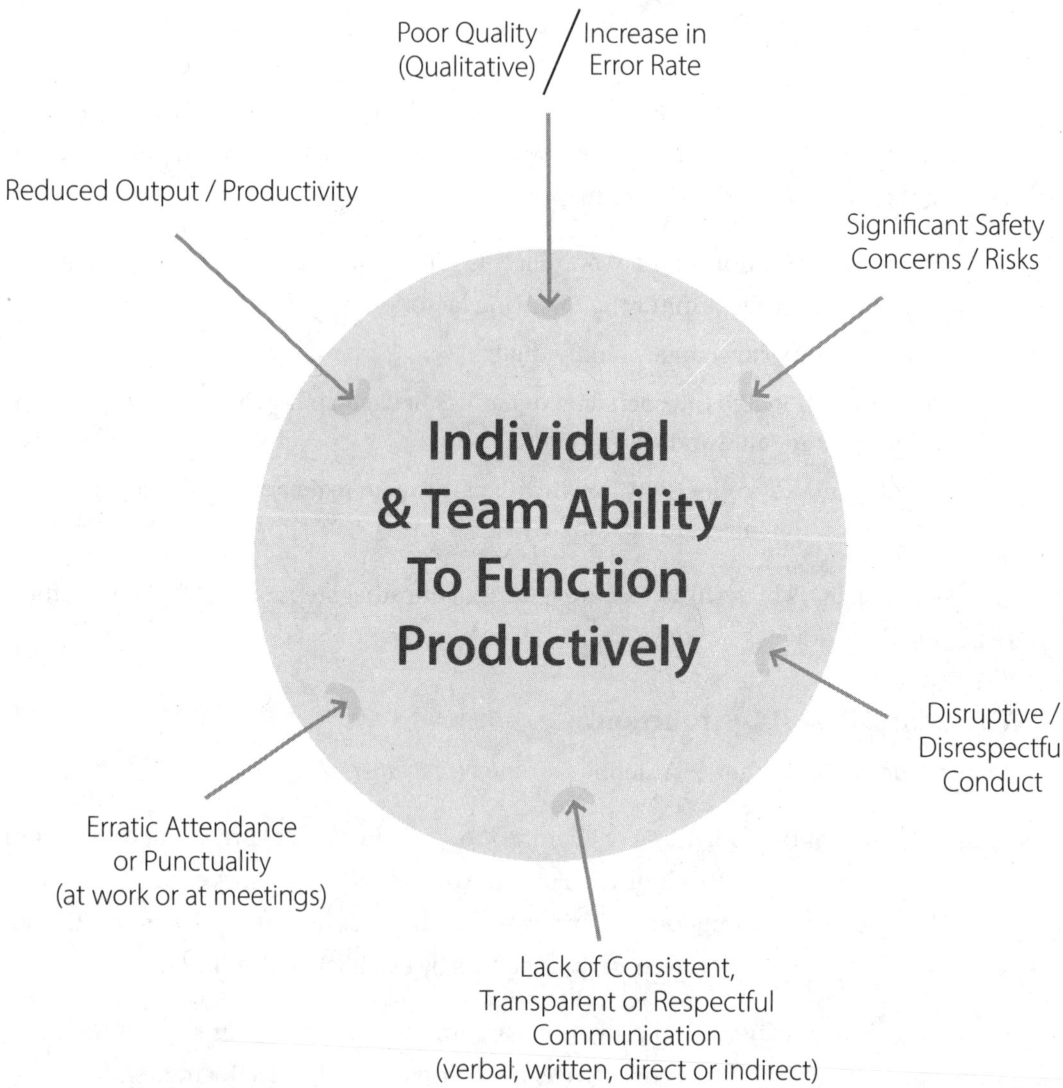

Figure 2: Role of the Individual or Team in Workplace Dysfunction

permanent personality flaw of an individual or the fixed state of a team, and should not be characterized or treated in this manner.

In other words, a DOT is simply an acknowledgment that something about the current situation is *not working* and needs to be fixed.

The Role of the Leader

A team can't function properly if one or more of its leaders behave in a way that is seen as dysfunctional, or in a way that interferes with the team's ability to meet its mandate.

Figure 3, Role of the Leader in Workplace Dysfunction, outlines DOTs of dysfunction relating to leaders. These include: perceptions of preferential treatment, inconsistent or unclear direction, lack of consultation with the team, lack of feedback to the team, lack of accountability, and micromanagement.

DOTs can include:

- Dysfunctional behavior, performance, or attendance by team members or leaders
- Disrespectful communication or disruptive behavior by team members or leaders
- Dysfunctional behavior between members of the same team or different teams
- Dysfunction between team members and third parties, including clients, consumers and the public
- Dysfunction among the whole team

In larger organizations, DOTs can also involve dysfunction between entire teams and departments.

For the purposes of Monitoring dysfunction, the root cause of the dysfunction is not relevant. At this stage, it doesn't matter if the potential dysfunction is seen as intentional or falling outside the person's control. All that matters is that the DOT is interfering with the ability of an individual or team to function properly.

Where to Start? Obtaining a Baseline of Performance

Workplace leaders are expected to interact and work with their teams on an ongoing basis to see if they are functioning well. It is not acceptable to wait for a specific incident to arise – by that point, unnecessary damage has already occurred. Proactive Monitoring of your team helps detect and resolve dysfunction in its early stages.

Role of the Leader in Workplace Dysfunction

M
Monitoring

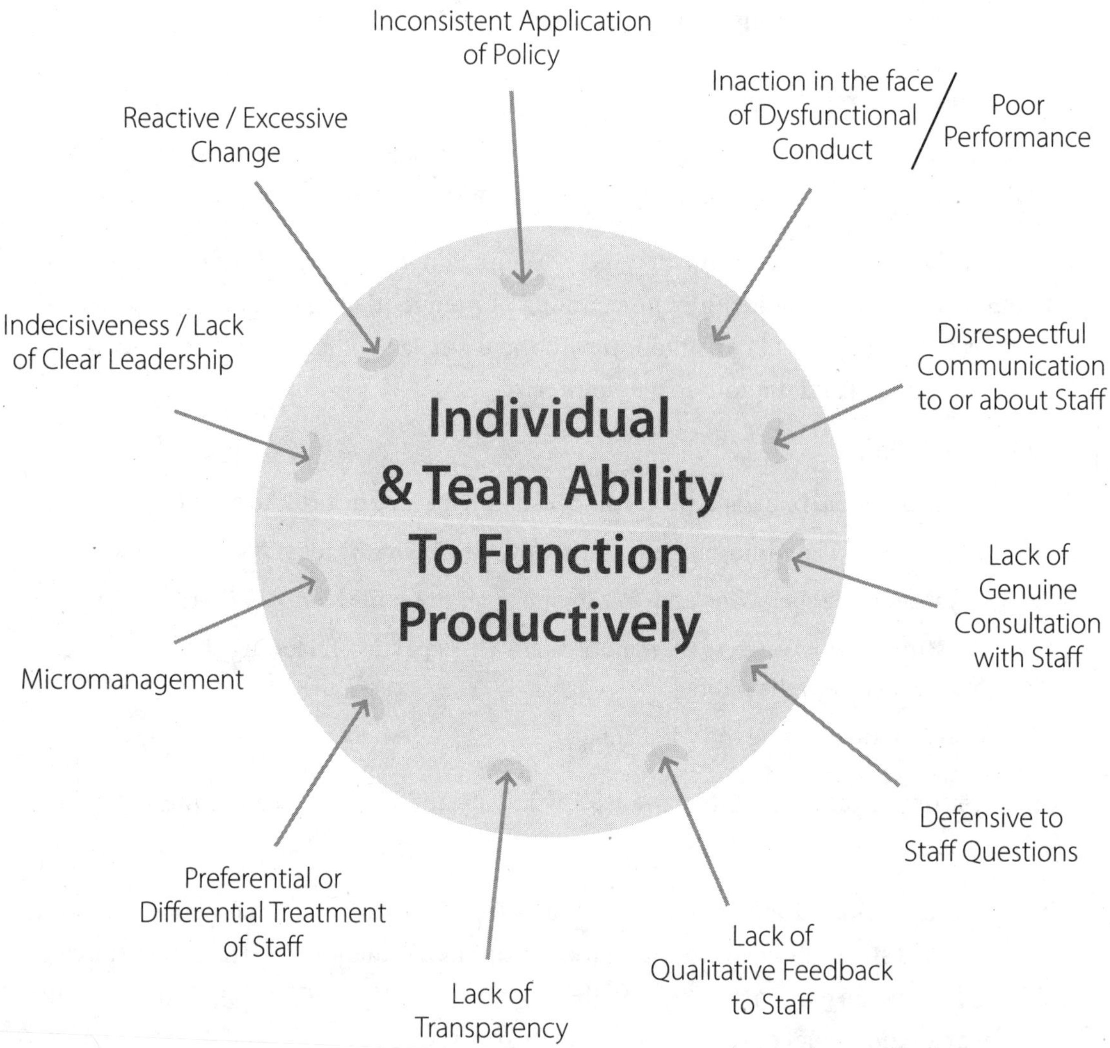

Figure 3: Role of the Leader in Workplace Dysfunction

Being aware of your team's ongoing health is a core duty for any leader. When you know how your team operates, you can quickly detect when and why things aren't working well and make adjustments as soon as possible.

Figure 4 is a Team Snapshot Form for assessing how individuals on your team, and how the team as a whole, are functioning. You should gather information in this form for each individual and team who report to you.

As with any tool in this workbook, you can and should modify these general suggestions to include specific criteria for your workplace and any general requirements that exist in your region or jurisdiction.

Before completing the Team Snapshot Form, review the job descriptions and profiles of each position on the team to remind yourself of the defined duties and expectations of individual team members, and gather additional information (from senior leaders perhaps), to better understand the overall mandate of the team.

Next, ask the following questions in relation to each team and team member, including any leaders who report to you:

- Are there past or current concerns with their ability to consistently show up and perform their work in an accurate and timely manner?
- Are there past or current concerns with their ability to interact, communicate or treat others with civility and respect?
- What are the team's rates of turnover (generally and compared to other departments)?
- What are the team's rates of sick leave, workers compensation, disability claims (generally and compared to other departments)?
- Are there any other specific and relevant team metrics available related to matters such as safety incidents, significant errors, negligence claims, or customer, patient, or student complaints?

We recognize that workplace leaders have been supervising their teams well before they learned of the MIRROR Method. They are not starting with a brand-new team. Supervisors newly trained in the MIRROR Method commonly ask, "Where do I begin?" A performance baseline like this is the answer to this question. It helps leaders apply the MIRROR Method to their current teams by providing them with a solid foundation on which to Monitor for and detect current DOTs in an informed manner.

Team Snapshot Form

M
Monitoring

A. General Baseline of Individual Performance

1. **Name of Employee** (Senior Leaders to include Managers and Supervisors in this Assessment)

2. **Any past reported or observed concerns re Individual Job Performance?** Circle all that might apply:

Productivity Accuracy Safe Practices Documentation

Customer Service (incl. public, patients, students, family, clients) Other (specify) ______________________

3. **Any past reported or observed concerns re Reliability as a Team Player?** Circle all that might apply:

Attendance Punctuality Trustworthiness Assisting Coworkers

Information Sharing & General Transparency Respect for Supervisory Authority & Direction

Respectful Workplace Communication (gossip, verbal and/or non-verbal disrespect)

Tolerance & Respect for Diversity (in work preferences and individual background)

Other (specify) ______________________

4. **If YES:**

Has employee been made aware of these issues/concerns? Yes / No (circle one)

Is employee on a formal performance improvement plan/progressive disciplinary track? Yes / No (circle one)

B. General Baseline of Team Performance

1. **Any observations or available metrics regarding the rate of turnover (including resignations and internal transfers), in general and as compared to other departments?**

2. **Any observations or available metrics regarding the rate of sick leave (including Workers Compensation and disability leaves) in general and as compared to other departments?**

Figure 4: Team Snapshot Form

M
Monitoring

CASE STUDY: TAKING THE TEAM SNAPSHOT AT DOLLARBILLS INC.

Preferably, you as an HR manager already have a baseline of this team's functioning *before* Joe comes forward with his complaint.

Using the Team Snapshot Form, you've recorded a baseline on this team that reflects:

- Prior complaints about Mike's communication with others, perhaps those who challenge him, new employees, or both
- Prior concerns or complaints about Mike or others not following mandatory regulatory or reporting practices
- Prior complaints or observations of Joe reacting to or refusing to follow the direction of senior staff/workplace leaders when he disagrees with their direction
- Prior complaints about Joe publicly discussing workplace disputes or concerns on social media or otherwise
- Prior complaints about Joe not adhering to hours of work or communicating properly with his supervisors
- Prior complaints about Joe unreasonably challenging current internal standards and practices
- Prior complaints or concerns about Laurie having personal relationships with certain staff, resulting in a perception of favoritism or bias
- Prior complaints or concerns about Laurie not effectively responding to or resolving complaints amongst staff

As part of this baseline, you should have on record this team's rates of turnover and sick leave. Even if the rates are low, you should look at the rate of turnover in Joe's position itself to determine if there are any patterns or trends of concern. You can compare these rates with turnover in other positions, prior years and other departments.

Finally, you can uncover if there have been concerns, questions or complaints into this department's regulatory or reporting practices. You should be aware of the details associated with these. When did they happen? What were the results? Were there any recommendations? Were they implemented?

How to Monitor for Current DOTs

The baseline assessment itself may highlight issues with individuals that demand your attention now. You should not wait for an incident to happen if your baseline assessment shows current concerns with the performance, communication or behavior of certain team members or reflects an active dispute between individuals or teams.

M
Monitoring

If your baseline reflects DOTs of dysfunction, then initiate the remaining steps of the MIRROR Method.

If the baseline assessment reflects a functioning team with functioning individuals, then you simply need to actively Monitor the team moving forward.

Monitor for DOTs on a continuing basis by:

- Observing your team in the workplace, in specific meetings, and on email
- Talking to your team in staff meetings, one-on-one discussions, performance reviews, and exit interviews
- Monitoring team and interpersonal communication in staff meetings, lunchrooms, office dynamics, and emails

Some examples of dysfunction you may observe when Monitoring the workplace include:

- Distancing of certain individuals, or cliquey behavior among certain subsets of the team
- Side-chats and whispering
- Over-inclusion or notable exclusion of certain individuals in relation to email exchanges or in-person meetings
- Disengagement of and active "shutting down" by certain individuals (this may be a change in their behavior)
- Dismissive or contemptuous comments or facial expressions, dramatic sighing and other non-verbal behavior
- Sarcastic laughter or comments not genuinely exhibited in jest
- Interrupting of others
- Dismissing others
- Talking over others
- Personalized attacks of others
- Prematurely exiting or ending communication in a dramatic manner to "send" a message to others

How *Not* to Monitor for DOTs

When Monitoring for DOTs, refrain from:

- Asking staff to Monitor other staff for performance, attendance, or behavioral issues, unless they are a designated mentor or acting supervisor, and the Monitoring is done in a transparent manner
- Asking staff general questions about the performance of other specific staff unless these questions take place as part of a formal performance Review or investigation of which the person is aware
- Disclosing your frustrations about a staff member's performance or behavior to other staff
- Informing staff that a staff member's performance or behavior is being Monitored
- Asking staff to confirm or corroborate the leader's suspicions or specific concerns about another staff member

Any DOTs from staff should come from them, unprompted and at their own initiative, or through open-ended questions posed during a Review.

Now What? Dealing with It at the DOT

The MIRROR Method emphasizes the importance of dealing with workplace dysfunction "at the DOT"—in other words, as soon as it appears no matter how trivial it may seem. Inaction in the face of dysfunction will create a train wreck of mistrust and strained communication over time, (see Figure 5, Dealing with it at the DOT) resulting in significant personal and professional costs to many on the team.

"Dealing with it at the DOT" does not mean you should immediately take action against an individual in response to concerns about that person's behavior.

It means you need to engage the next steps of the MIRROR Method whenever a DOT appears. In fact, if the MIRROR Method is not triggered after a leader has learned of a DOT, then the leader may be seen as responsible for any ongoing, subsequent workplace dysfunction.

What's Next

In Step 2, you'll learn how to:

- Triage DOTs of dysfunction by gathering information, deciding on the type of Review required, and identifying who should conduct the Review

Dealing with it at the DOT

Dysfunction on Team

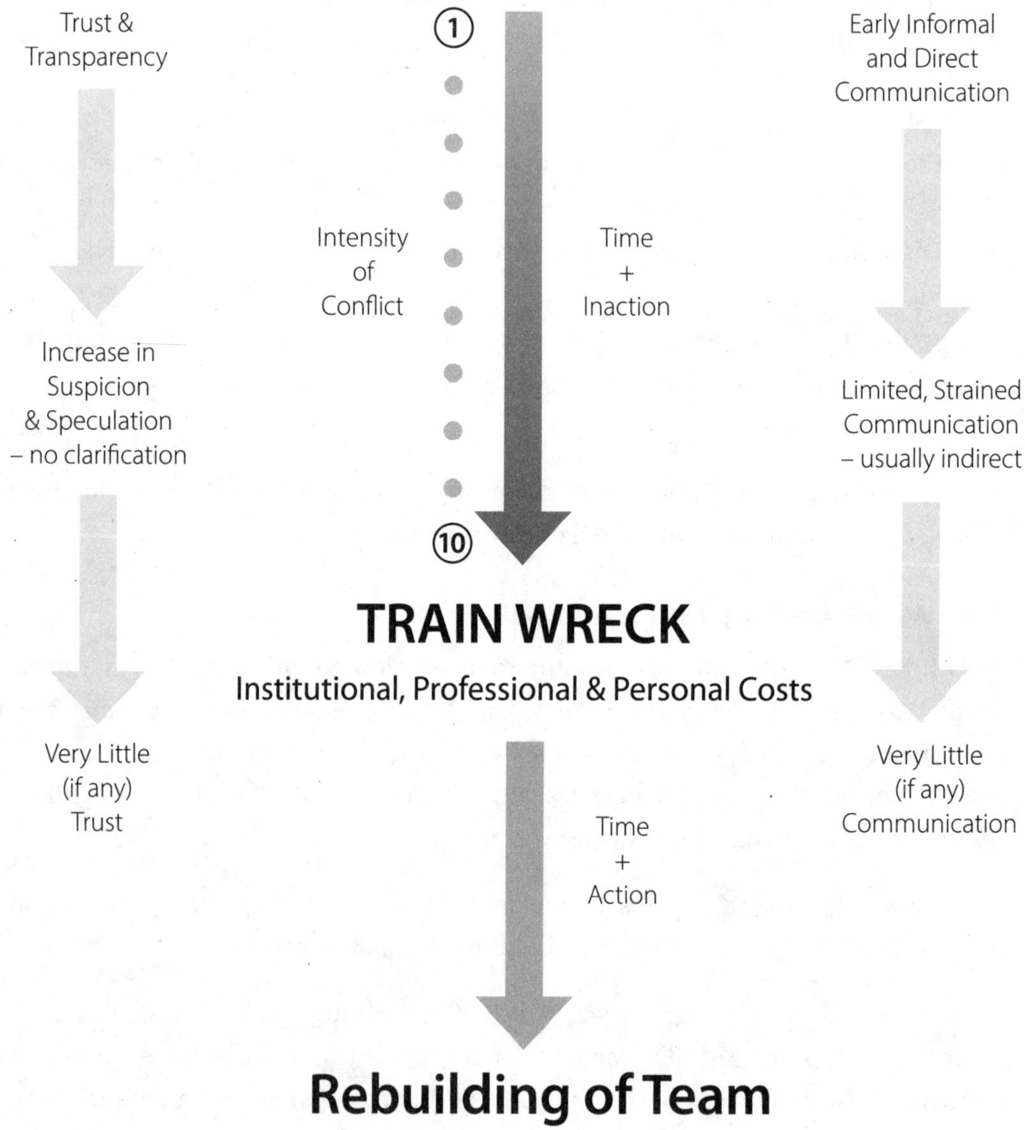

Figure 5: Dealing with it at the DOT

M

Monitoring

STEP 2 — INQUIRING INTO THE DOT

Once a DOT comes to a leader's attention, the question most commonly asked is "Now what do I do?"

Step 2, Inquiring into the DOT, is the "I" of the MIRROR Method and helps leaders answer this question.

I
Inquire

Leaders must assess the potential seriousness of the alleged dysfunction to determine the best next step. Can they Review the situation informally or do the allegations require a formal investigation?

Next steps should not be influenced by personal opinion, prejudgment, favoritism, or fear. They should be determined by objectively considering the allegations that have come forward to determine the potential seriousness of this situation.

This is called the Triage Process.

What is the Triage Process?

The term *Triage* is adopted from the medical community. When individuals arrive at the Emergency room, they are initially assessed (or Triaged), to determine the potential severity of their reported symptoms. Cases Triaged as severe are investigated sooner and more aggressively than those Triaged as mild.

Using this concept as a leader, you need to assess the potential severity of the workplace complaint or concern before determining the scope and nature of your intervention.

Figure 6, The Triage Process, shows the Scale of Dysfunctional Conduct (on a scale of 1 to 10), on which any given DOT might fall. Complaints that appear to be relatively recent and mild in nature should be Triaged on the "bad day" end of the scale (resulting in informal interventions), while those that appear long-standing, repetitive or serious in nature should be Triaged on the "bad life" end of the scale (requiring formal Reviews or investigations).

Investigations and interventions are discussed in detail below and in Step 3, Conducting the Review. For now, it is enough to know that informal Reviews do not result in formal discipline of anyone involved. They're instead used to clarify future expectations

The Triage Process

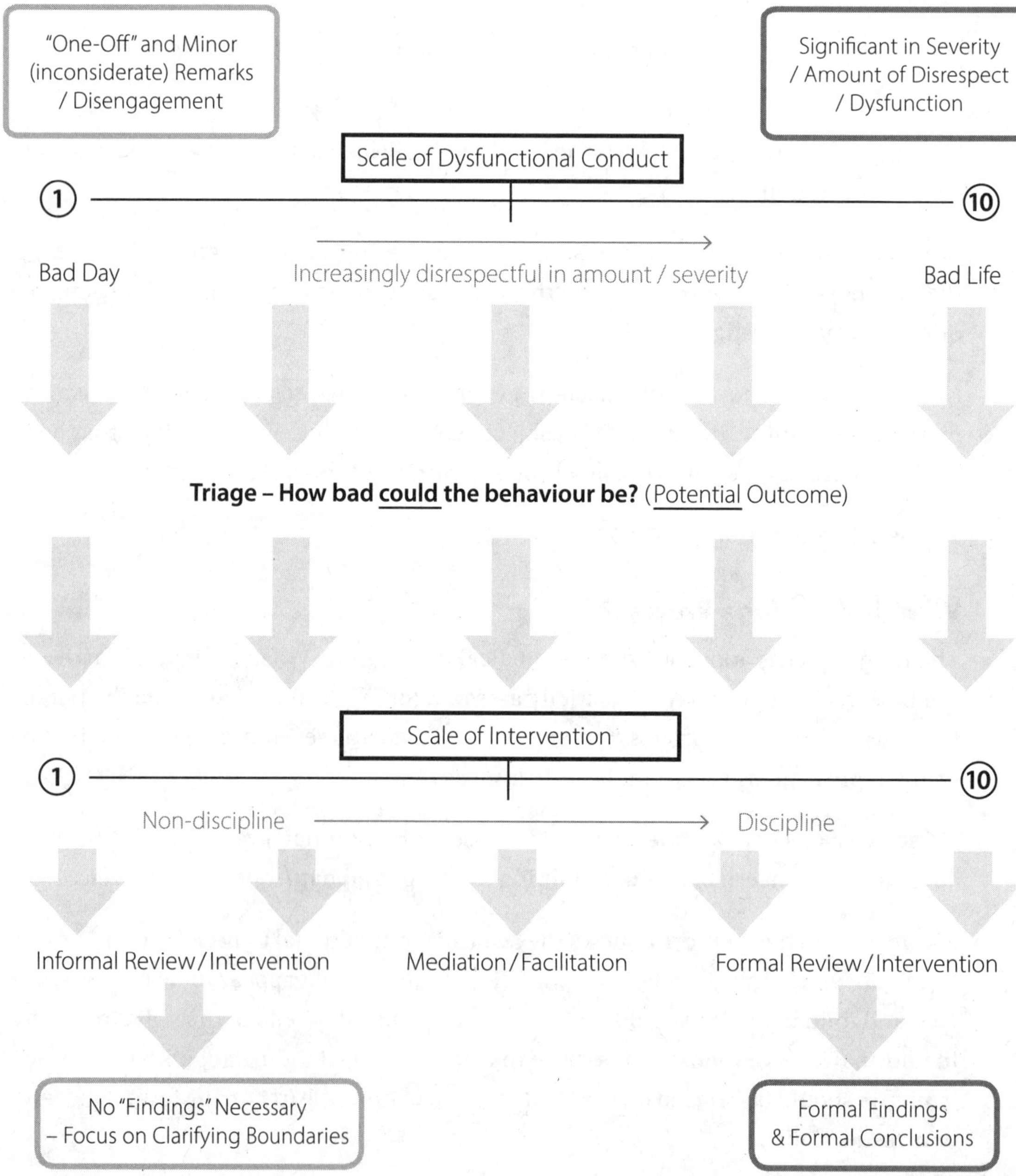

Figure 6: The Triage Process

and boundaries using one-on-one discussions and various types of mediations and facilitations. Formal Reviews commonly result in findings of fault against and formal discipline of individuals, up to termination of employment, and therefore demand a far more stringent, rigid and technical process to ensure due diligence.

Figure 7 is a Real-time Complaint Form to help you with the Triage Process. There are two different components to it: the first part applies to reports received by leaders, and the other applies to observations made by leaders. The information from the checklist will help leaders Triage the DOT to determine whether it warrants an informal or formal Review.

1. Gathering Information

Leaders often observe or hear of a DOT during a general discussion, in a brief email, or through a one-off comment or remark.

Once a leader observes, hears, or learns of a possible DOT about or between team members, there is an obligation to follow-up on the possible issue to determine next steps.

2. Deconstructing Labels

When gathering information, you often hear people using general characterizations to describe their concerns about someone else. For example, they may say someone is: unproductive, incompetent, disengaged, bullying, aggressive, and so on.

These references and assertions cannot be properly Triaged because they are labels. Everyone uses, interprets and understands labels in different ways.

For this reason, when completing the form, you need to deconstruct labels into specific behavior, communication, and performance issues of concern.

You can deconstruct labels by asking the following:

- What do you mean by "incompetent, disengaged, bullying"?
- What are the specific interactions, statements or behaviors that occurred that you view as "incompetent, disengaged, or bullying"?

In addition, when complaining about others, individuals often describe their own reactions and emotions in response to the alleged DOT. They report feeling anxious, intimidated, silenced, stressed, and so on. Just as labels of others' behaviors should not be Triaged, neither should the emotional reactions to those behaviors.

Real-time Complaint Form

The Duty to Inquire

1. **Name of Employee(s) / Team with Potential Issue**

2. **Nature of Concern?** Circle all that might apply:

   a. **Any past reported or observed concerns re Individual Job Performance?**

   Productivity   Accuracy   Safe Practices   Documentation

   Customer Service (incl. public, patients, students, family, clients)   Other (specify) ____________

   b. **Any past reported or observed concerns re Reliability as a Team Player?**

   Attendance   Punctuality   Trustworthiness   Assisting Coworkers

   Information Sharing & General Transparency   Respect for Supervisory Authority & Direction

   Respectful Workplace Communication (gossip, verbal and/or non-verbal disrespect)

   Tolerance & Respect for Diversity (in work preferences and individual background)

   Other (specify) ____________

3. **Source of Concern?** Circle all that might apply:

   Reported to Leader   Observed by Workplace Leader   Other (specify) ____________

4. **If Reported to a Leader:**

   a. **Who reported complaint?**

   Name:

   Relationship to Organization: Circle one

   Employee   Leader   Other (specify) ____________
   (e.g. Customer, Supplier, Member of Public, etc.)

   Contact Information:

Figure 7: Real-time Complaint Form

4. **cont'd:**

b. **Outline what was reported:** Fill in below and/or attach a copy of the text/email

c. **Outline any background that is potentially relevant to the concern (e.g. prior concerns, prior history):**
Fill in below and/or attach additional notes

d. **Outline any direct steps taken by individual before reporting the concern and the response by the subject employee (including his/her demeanor to the feedback):** Fill in below and/or attach additional notes

Figure 7: Real-time Complaint Form continued

Inquire

5. If directly observed by the workplace leader:

   a. Outline what was specifically witnessed including what was heard and why it was of concern (if not readily apparent to a layperson). Include a description of behaviors, not a label, judgment or characterization of those behaviors (e.g. state that "he/she was speaking with a loud voice with a red face and a stern expression" NOT "he was speaking inappropriately or aggressively or angrily"): Fill in below and/or attach additional notes

   b. Outline any relevant background in relation to this situation (relevant history of the individuals involved, prior expectations to the subject employee, similar past complaints): Fill in below and/or attach additional notes

   c. Outline any immediate discussions or other steps taken in response to the observed concern: Fill in below and/or attach additional notes

NONE yet, or:

Figure 7: Real-time Complaint Form continued

Instead, those emotions should be deconstructed as follows:

- What specific interaction, communication or behavior involving this other person has caused you to feel anxious or intimidated?
- In what specific way did you find the person's behavior or communication to be intimidating or stressful? What about their behavior triggered your reaction?

The Real-time Complaint Form should include the specific behaviors, communication practices and performance issues you gathered *after* deconstructing general labels and broad characterizations. You cannot determine next steps without them.

In addition, you should gather the following details about the alleged complaint or concerns:

- When did these incidents, events, or discussions happen? Are they historical or recent?
- How often has this or something similar occurred with this person? Is this something new? Is this a recent change in the person's behavior or performance or has it become the norm for how this person operates?
- How seriously has this impacted the individual's or team's ability to function? In what ways?

After gathering this information, you should advise the person who has come forward that their information will be considered in determining next steps. However, you should refrain from making any preliminary judgments about the alleged concerns or committing to taking any action at this stage, even if pressured to do so.

CASE STUDY: COMPLETING THE REAL-TIME COMPLAINT FORM FOR JOE'S ISSUE

In the case study, there are two occasions on which the form should be completed.

1. When Joe first approached Laurie with his concerns. Laurie (on her own or with HR) should have met with Joe confidentially to obtain more information about his concerns. Using the form, Laurie could have asked Joe for specific examples of concerns regarding:

- Non-compliance with regulatory/reporting practices (which are broad characterizations)
- Details on Mike's interactions with him

Inquire

Each DOT (in this case, the specific regulatory issues and the Mike issue) should be canvassed separately by Laurie by obtaining more information about each as follows:

- The specific alleged infractions (what was said, what was done, what was the context)
- How often have the alleged concerns (statements or actions) taken place (one-off, daily, weekly, intermittently, etc.)
- The impact on Joe's ability to work or the team's ability to properly meet its mandate
- Whether Joe previously raised these concerns with others. If so, who and what happened, and if not, why
- Any other information or history that might come up that may be relevant to this situation

2. When Joe contacted you in HR. You should complete the form with information from Joe, Laurie, and other leaders in the department. In addition to the DOT regarding the regulatory issues and DOT regarding Mike, other DOTs to Triage now include:

- Laurie's supervision, including any perceived allegiance or connection with the senior group
- The reasonableness of Laurie's earlier response to Joe's concern
- Joe feeling dismissed by the team (a label that needs to be deconstructed)
- The Facebook post by Joe
- Perceived shunning and retaliation against Joe by the group (again, these are broad characterizations)
- Joe's early departure from work without notification

To complete this process, the very same questions posed in relation to the two initial issues (regulatory practices and Mike's comment) need to be canvassed in relation to these other matters. Given that Laurie is now involved as a potential contributor to the DOT issues, she should not be involved in the Triage Process or any other steps of the MIRROR Method for this particular Review.

The Real-Time Complaint form should be completed for each issue.

For the purposes of this case study, assume that Laurie did not seek information from Joe when he initially approached her.

3. Determining the Type of Review

After gathering and recording additional information on the form, you should Triage the DOTs based on their potential seriousness.

In doing so, you should ask:

- If the allegations are found to be true, where would they fall on the Scale of Dysfunctional Conduct?
- Are they more in line with the mild and infrequent behavior that falls at the "bad day" end of the scale or the severe or frequent behavior that falls at the "bad life" end of the scale? Perhaps somewhere in-between?

Or, put another way, if the allegations are true, could they:

- Result in formal discipline, including dismissal, of the individuals involved?
- Result in adverse media coverage for the individuals and/or the organization?
- Result in safety, labor, civil or criminal litigation for individuals and/or the organization?
- Attract the attention of regulatory agencies overseeing the individuals or organization?
- Adversely affect the overall reputation of the organization, if brought to the attention of the public?

If the answer to any of these questions is *yes*, you should conduct a formal Review. If the answer is *no*, then you may be able to resolve the matter using an informal approach depending on the disciplinary and other history of the individuals involved.

The Review Decision Tree shown in Figure 8 is a tool to help you decide which Review path to choose. It also identifies which type of neutral party (internal or external) should conduct the Review.

In general, frontline workplace leaders and middle managers, with the assistance of HR, may oversee informal processes if they have not been involved in the events relating to the DOT under Review. If a frontline leader has been directly involved, then it is appropriate for a different workplace leader or HR advisor to facilitate the informal Review and resolution.

Formal Reviews should be conducted by senior managers, senior HR professionals, or external consultants, depending on the situation. Formal Reviews and investigations are now routinely scrutinized by adjudicators for procedural fairness and objectivity, so it is imperative to retain an experienced, credible investigator.

As always, specific decisions surrounding what Review to conduct and who should conduct it depend on the unique procedural, legal and other requirements of your organization and the jurisdiction in which you operate.

I
Inquire

CASE STUDY: TRIAGING JOE'S COMPLAINT

In the real world, it would be impossible and irresponsible to Triage the case study on the facts presented. As it reads (which is similar to initial reports leaders often receive), it lacks details on the nature or frequency of the various incidents.

For example, if Mike has no history with Joe and this is the first comment he has made, then this should be an informal Review. Why? Because if this is the first incident, then even if it is found to have been inappropriate, it would not warrant formal discipline. However, if this comment is part of a long-standing pattern of comments made by Mike (to Joe or to others) and/or if Mike is already on a performance management program or involved with progressive discipline, then it needs to be a formal Review, even if this one incident—standing alone—might appear to be mild.

The same applies to every other DOT. If this was the first time Laurie heard from Joe, then an informal Review of her response to him will be sufficient. However, if Joe reports that he had outlined prior concerns to her with no or a limited response, then a more formal Review of her supervisory practices will need to be invoked.

What about Joe's Facebook post and decision to leave early without notifying anyone?

The fact that Joe came forward to complain about others does not immunize him from being held accountable for any inappropriate workplace behavior and communication on his part. This too will need to be done using the MIRROR Method. In this context, Joe will need to be questioned not only about his complaints but also about his own conduct during these events.

Whether this will be done informally or formally depends on: how serious his Facebook post is; whether he has posted more than once; whether he had been warned about inappropriate use of social media previously; and similarly, the frequency and seriousness of this and any other early departures from work. If both appear to be relatively mild infractions that have occurred infrequently, then his DOTs may be Reviewed informally. Otherwise, he will be required to undergo a formal Review.

Review Decision Tree

Selecting the Process

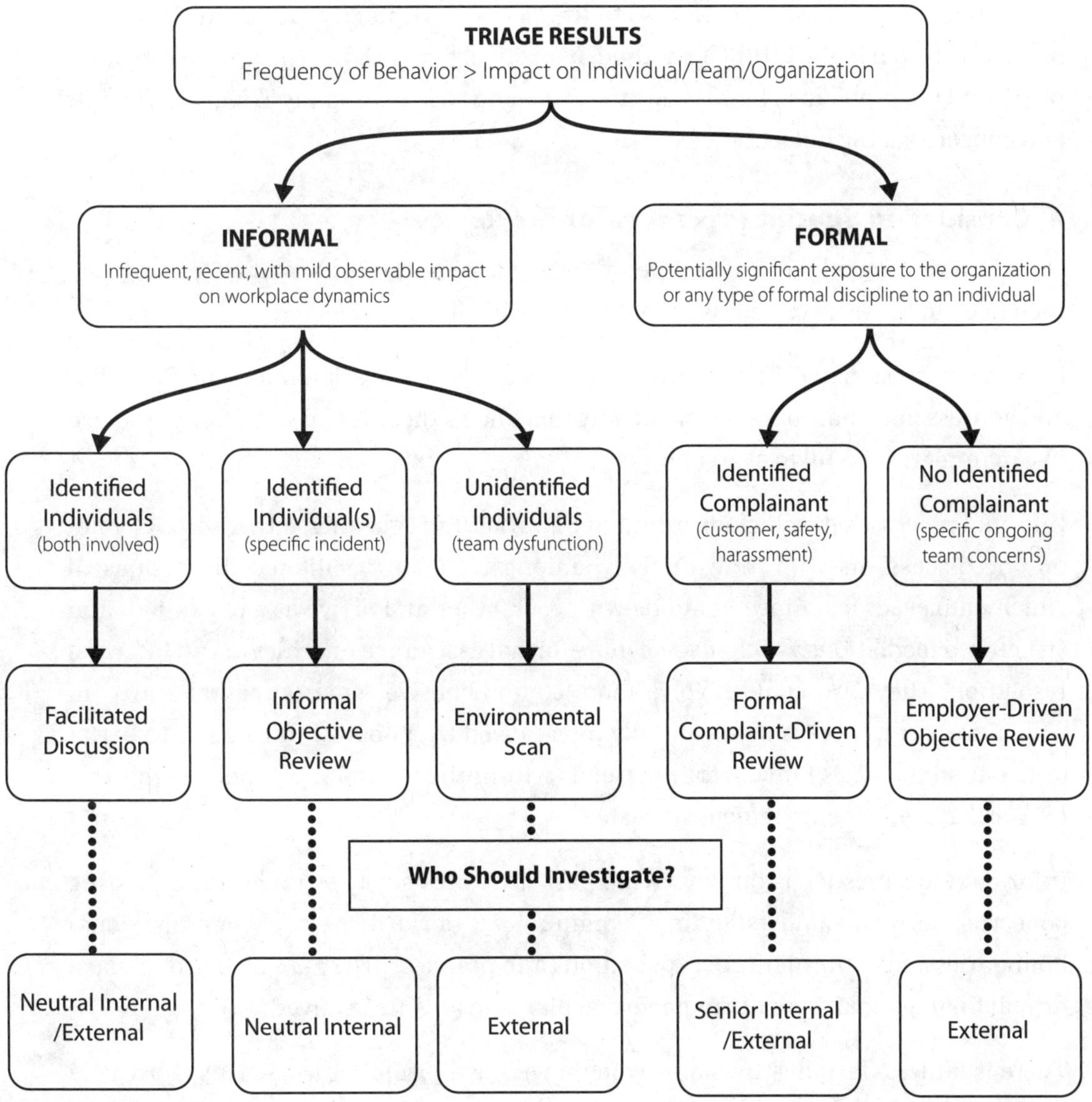

Figure 8: Review Decision Tree

The Triage Process is often overlooked in many workplaces. Instead, there is a "one size fits all" approach based on the complaint as initially reported.

The application of the Triage Process to the case study should make clear the importance of this step in the MIRROR Method. It's critical to match the specific investigative process to the problem at hand. The only way to do so is to properly Triage complaints and concerns at the outset.

4. Considering Specific Processes for the Review

Once you've determined which type of Review is required (informal or formal), you then need to consider various ways in which each may be conducted.

Informal processes may be customized and creative. Leaders can intervene to Review and address informal concerns in any way that allows these issues to be fairly resolved in a manner respectful to everyone.

Informal processes may include informal inquiries and coaching, either through one-on-one discussions with individuals or amongst a team; facilitated discussions in which employees examine situations with each other and arrive at a resolution; and structured mediations which involve more formal assistance in achieving an informal resolution. They also could involve more comprehensive "environmental scans" in which every employee is confidentially interviewed by a neutral third party to better understand the basis for concerning trends within the team (for example, high turnover/sick leave, low engagement scores).

Informal processes focus on Reviewing past situations solely to understand existing concerns, clarify misunderstandings, communicate or clarify personal or professional boundaries and confirm future expectations and practices. They are not used to make formal findings against or attribute formal blame to anyone involved.

There is far less flexibility available when invoking a formal process. This is because formal Reviews often result in adverse employment and other consequences to individuals (such as revocation or suspension of professional licenses or privileges). To ensure these consequences are based upon accurate findings against those involved, various jurisdictions and workplaces have established specific and rigid processes to follow when conducting formal investigations and Reviews. This is so regardless of whether the formal Reviews are triggered by complaints from fellow employees (for example, harassment complaints), or complaints from employers (for example, misconduct or safety complaints).

What's Next

In Step 3, you'll learn how to:

- Conduct a Review, which includes setting up the Review, gathering information appropriately and objectively, making findings, and reaching conclusions

Inquire

STEP 3 — CONDUCTING THE REVIEW

In Step 2, you used the Triage Process to determine whether to conduct an informal or formal Review. In Step 3, we'll outline a framework to follow when conducting these Reviews.

Key Principles

Both informal and formal Reviews should be:

- Started and completed in a timely manner
- Objective and balanced, in that they include and consider information from everyone involved
- Neutral, in that the person conducting the Review is seen as unbiased

R
Review

Informal Reviews

Informal Reviews are suitable for concerns or allegations that, if proven, would not warrant formal discipline or significant intervention.

The purpose of an informal Review is to better understand "what happened" at a specific time, disclose concerns or misunderstandings that have arisen and communicate clearer expectations and boundaries for the future. Often, both or all of the individuals involved end up receiving feedback about their specific role in the dynamics as well as some constructive direction on how to move forward.

Informal interventions and Reviews can be accomplished in several ways. You can:

- Encourage and coach individuals to try to resolve an issue on their own by speaking directly with those with whom they have a concern.
- Help facilitate a meeting between individuals to allow them to share their experiences and perspectives in relation to a specific incident or interaction and then work with them to resolve the situation. If they are unable to come to a mutually agreeable resolution, you would give each of them guidance or expectations (as necessary) for moving forward based on what you heard and observed during the process.
- Meet with your team to outline and remind everyone of general expectations moving forward (this is used most effectively when the issue seems to have come up repeatedly with different staff members).

- If individuals are not open to meeting together, either on their own or with you in attendance, then you should resolve the matter informally by having brief one-on-one meetings with each person to listen to their perspective, gather any relevant information you need to fully understand what happened, and then, after considering all the information, determine what most likely happened and how best to proceed. This process is very similar to the formal process, set out below, but is applied on a smaller scale and in a more expedited manner.

Formal Reviews

Setting Up the Review

A defensible Review starts well before your first witness.

To set up the Review for success, be sure to complete Checklist A: Setting up the Review shown in Figure 9 as well as any other steps required in your particular workplace/jurisdiction.

R
Review

Each factor in the Checklist is discussed at length in *The Mirror Method* book.

Checklist A: Setting up the Review

Factors to Consider

Factors To Consider	✓	**Date(s)** (if applicable)
Have the necessary parties/individuals been informed of the review?		
Has each individual been cautioned about confidentiality and retaliation?		
Have interim measures (transfers/suspensions of certain individuals/adjustment of reporting structure) been considered and if necessary implemented?		
Has the appropriate investigator (experienced, neutral) been retained?		
Has the investigator been given instructions on scope and timing of investigation?		
Has the appropriate venue been considered and selected (on/off-site)?		
Has requested or mandated representation been arranged?		
Have all other relevant procedural requirements in specific collective agreements, workplace policies and contracts been met?		

Figure 9: Checklist A: Setting up the Review

Conducting the Review

When conducting your Review, interview everyone with potentially relevant information about the matters being investigated, including the respondent/accused, to determine:

- What specifically happened? What was said? What was done? In what context?
- Who was involved?
- Where did this take place?
- When did this take place?
- Why did they respond (or not respond) in the way and manner they did?
- How did each person act, speak or interact at the time? This includes verbal and non-verbal behavior.

Use Checklist B: Conducting the Review shown in Figure 10 as a guideline for your information-gathering process. Again, you may need to consider and include additional customized steps, based on the issue being investigated, the requirements of your workplace and the laws that govern the jurisdiction in which you operate.

R
Review

Possible Questions to Consider

Checklist C: Review Questions shown in Figure 11 provides you with sample questions you may wish to ask. These are only suggestions and, at most, a good place to begin. Your questions need to be customized based on the issues under Review, the applicable workplace policies and procedures and the information you have gathered to date.

During any interview, be ready and prepared to ask additional questions on the fly based on the person's responses to your questions. A pre-determined rigid list of questions will interfere with your ability to obtain all the necessary information.

When conducting your interviews, it is important to treat each individual in a respectful and professional manner. Workplace investigations are not interrogations and should not be conducted in an aggressive or hostile way.

Checklist B: Conducting the Review

Conducting the Interview - General Principles	✓	**Date(s)** (if applicable)
Each individual has been told (again) about confidentiality and non-retaliation		
Each witness has been advised of the importance of being open and honest		
All particulars (who, what, when, where) about each reported "concern"/event are canvassed with all relevant individuals (witnesses and parties)		
Questions are **open-ended** and **open-minded**		
All labels are 'broken down' into specific behaviors, actions or statements (e.g. what did the person mean by "unsafe" – what behaviors/communication did they see as unsafe? Or, what did they mean by aggressive or intimidating? What were the demonstrable behaviors or statements of concern?)		
Any and all potentially relevant documents are obtained and reviewed (e.g. emails, letters, available Facebook posts, texts, timecards, expense reports, logs, receipts, complaint forms, manager's notes, etc.)		
Disrespectful or other notable behavior during the interview is documented and if necessary, addressed at the time		
After interviewing complainant and his/her witnesses, interview the accused		
If the responses from the accused differ from those you obtained during the course of the investigation, put the information/discrepancy to the accused and ask for a response		
Do not "hide" anything from the accused. Give him/her an opportunity to consider the particulars of the concerns against him/her as well as time to respond and explain his/her perspective		
Interview witnesses relevant to the accused's version of events		
Re-interview specific individuals, if necessary, to effectively consider evidence/explanations from accused		
Complete a process timeline throughout the investigation (e.g. steps taken, date/time/name of the individual interviewed, documents requested/obtained/reviewed)		
Take and date neutral, factual notes of interviews		

Figure 10: Checklist B: Conducting the Review

Conducting the Interview	✓	Date(s) (if applicable)
Include non-verbal behaviors in interview in the notes (e.g. long pauses, sighing, laughing sarcastically, remorse, crying, anger etc.).		
Prepare Summaries of Evidence based on Interview notes		
Make Findings of fact based on the assessment of all of the evidence and credibility of those interviewed		
Draw conclusions as to whether any relevant legislation/policy/procedure has been breached (based on the Findings of Fact)		
If part of the mandate, develop recommendations		

Figure 10: Checklist B: Conducting the Review continued

Checklist C: Review Questions

Sample Questions to Consider Not Exhaustive - Please Customize	✓
What happened?	
Describe what it looked like to you?	
When did it/they happen?	
Who was present?	
Who did or said what (including you)?	
In what order?	
Is there any notes/documents?	
Who else may have relevant information? Explain	
What happened afterwards?	
Who did you speak with? What did you say?	
Why was there a delay in reporting the incident(s)/concern(s) (if applicable)? Explain	
What has been the impact on the person at work?	
Is there anything else you think I should know?	
Is there anything that you think is important that I may have missed?	

If there is more than one allegation/incident, ask the questions set out above again.

Possible Additional Questions for the Accused Fill in below and/or attach additional notes/questions	✓

Figure 11: Checklist C: Review Questions

CASE STUDY: CONDUCTING THE REVIEW

As a manager in HR, you are charged with conducting the Review into Joe's complaint.

At the start of the Review, you ask Joe, using open-ended questions, to outline his overall experience at the workplace. This allows Joe to share his story in an unscripted manner, at his own pace and in his own words.

After he has finished his story, you then ask Joe directed and more specific questions about the specific regulatory practices of concern to him. In each incident, he should be asked to describe in detail what happened and why he thinks it is an issue.

You then ask Joe specific questions in response to any other issues he has raised, either in his written complaint or during his interview. This includes his concerns about Mike and Laurie.

At the end of the interview, you should have a clear understanding of Joe's concerns and allegations. If you remain confused or unclear about a particular issue, or any part of his story, then you need to ask Joe additional questions.

After interviewing Joe, you should interview other individuals that directly witnessed or have relevant information regarding the alleged incidents to determine what they saw, heard or did at the time. Use the same process with witnesses as you did with Joe. First, let them tell you their story and then follow up with specific questions.

You also need to gather and review all relevant documentation, such as logs, work schedules, work memoranda, emails, texts, regulatory policies, procedures and minutes from relevant staff meetings.

Repeat this process for each separate concern brought forward (by Joe or by others in relation to Joe).

Interviewing the Accused

After meeting with the person who raised the concerns or filed the complaint, and after interviewing relevant witnesses, you then need to interview the accused (who is also commonly referred to as a Respondent or Defendant).

Your interview with the accused should be very similar in structure and tone to your interviews with others. If you treat the accused differently (for example, by speaking to him or her in an accusatory or dismissive manner, or by interrupting or shutting him or her down), you will be vulnerable to a claim of bias or pre-judgment which will place the integrity of your findings and conclusions at risk.

As noted in the Checklist B: Conducting the Review (Figure 10), the accused should be given a full opportunity to share his or her perspective on what transpired. The accused should be made aware of all allegations and given an opportunity to fully respond to any evidence that points to wrongdoing.

Later on in the interview, the accused should be told of key differences between his or her story and the information provided by others and then should be given a chance to respond.

Following the accused's interview, you should collect documents and interview witnesses relevant to his or her explanation, and follow up on new information or assertions raised by the accused that are relevant to your Review. This may require re-interviewing the complainant or certain witnesses.

Findings and Conclusions

At the end of your Review, and based on all the information you have collected, you need to determine:

- What most likely happened at the time. In other words, make general **findings of fact** based on your assessment of the information provided.
- Whether what happened is objectively viewed as a violation of workplace policy or in some other way considered unreasonable or inappropriate. In other words, make **conclusions** about the findings you've made given the relevant legislation, workplace laws, policies and procedures.

Findings of Fact

In the case study example, if Joe's complaint is Reviewed formally, you would hear from relevant individuals, examine relevant documentation, and make specific findings of fact in relation to:

- Each regulatory concern raised by Joe
- Mike's apparent comments to Joe
- Laurie's response to Joe's concerns
- Possibly, Laurie's relationships or friendships with certain team members
- The Facebook post by Joe

- Alleged shunning of Joe
- Joe allegedly leaving early

Making Conclusions

After making these findings (that is, your determination of "what happened" in each instance), you need to apply the standards set out in workplace policies and procedures and legislation to *conclude* if any your findings constitute a violation of:

- Regulatory standards, practices and procedures
- Supervisory policies
- Codes of Conduct
- Hours of work and leave policies
- Workplace respect/harassment policies
- Human rights/anti-discrimination policies
- Social media policies
- Other relevant policies and procedures at this worksite

R
Review

CASE STUDY: MAKING FINDINGS AND CONCLUSIONS REGARDING A SPECIFIC ALLEGATION

Let's examine the allegation that in response to Joe raising regulatory concerns, Mike, a senior employee, said:

"Listen, Junior, you're not in college anymore. This is the real world. Just relax, watch and learn."

Mike might respond to this allegation as follows:

1. Mike could deny that he even made the statement. ("I've never said anything like that to anyone").
2. Mike could admit he said, "something like that" to Joe but "not in that way". For example, he may explain that Joe seemed overly concerned about every regulatory practice that appeared to depart from what he learned in college. Mike made this comment to Joe to lighten things up and help Joe move from theory into practice.
3. Mike could admit making the statement (exactly as framed by Joe) but state that, in his opinion, it was neither offensive nor inappropriate and Joe was being overly sensitive.
4. Mike could admit that his statement was inappropriate but assert that he was having personal issues at the time which clouded his judgment.

R
Review

Mike's explanations in paragraphs #1 and #2 would be considered when making your findings of fact. Specifically, you would determine whether Mike made the statement at all, and if so, in what manner or context. Based on all the information you gathered (including your assessment of Joe and Mike as witnesses, any related texts and emails, etc.), did you think Mike made the statement? If so, was Mike's manner genuine and supportive or sarcastic and dismissive?

If you find it most likely that the statement was not made at all, then you need to state this as a finding and dismiss this allegation against Mike.

If you find it most likely that Mike made this statement, then you then need to determine, as a finding of fact, how it was delivered and the tone that was used.

Assume, for the purpose of this case study, that you determined that Mike made this statement to Joe in a dismissive manner.

You then need to conclude if this statement, said in this way, violates any workplace laws, policies and/or procedures or is inconsistent with general community standards about appropriate workplace communication.

This is where Mike's potential explanation in paragraph #3 becomes relevant; Mike denies that his statement was offensive or inappropriate and defends himself on this basis.

In these circumstances, you need to ask whether a reasonable and informed person working in your community and jurisdiction – at the time the statement was made – would view Mike's statement as intimidating or offensive. This is not based on Joe's or Mike's *opinions or feelings* about the statement, it is based on how a reasonable person in similar circumstances would have interpreted and viewed this statement. This is often called the "Reasonable Person" test or standard.

Objective Reviews must be objectively and fairly conducted. The outcome of these Reviews must be rooted in evidence-based findings of fact and evidence-based, reasonable conclusions.

Objective Reviews cannot blindly validate or invalidate certain cultural or political perspectives that might exist in a workplace at a given time. Nor can they be based upon the emotional pleas of the "Joes" or the passionate denials of the "Mikes". The outcomes must be rooted in the objective evidence gathered during the Review process and reflective of the objective standards in force at the time – nothing less and nothing more.

If you determine that a reasonable person would not have viewed Mike's statement as "objectively or reasonably offensive" (considering *your findings* on both the words said and the context in which they were made), then you need to *conclude* that Mike's statement is not objectively inappropriate or offensive. This particular allegation would be dismissed.

If, however, you consider that a reasonable person would have viewed Mike's statement as "objectively or reasonably offensive", then you need to conclude that his statement is inappropriate and move to the next step of the MIRROR Method, Remedy, to devise an appropriate response.

In making this determination, it is important to consider any relevant definitions and principles outlined in workplace laws (for example, Human Rights or Workers Compensation legislation), and workplace-related Codes of Conduct, Respectful Workplace/ Harassment policies, Standards of Practice and otherwise. In ambiguous or complex cases, you also should consult with legal counsel to better understand the application of the "reasonable community standard" to your particular situation and jurisdiction given that this standard changes over time, as social and legal expectations evolve.

Mike may admit that he engaged in wrongdoing but attempt to justify his behavior based on personal issues or workplace dynamics at the time. This is reflected in his explanation in paragraph #4 above. Factors used to explain or excuse someone's actions ("I was overworked, sad, mad, hungry, tired, sick at the time") are not relevant to your findings of fact or your conclusions of wrongdoing. They are relevant to determining what action to take in response to the inappropriate conduct. This will be canvassed in the next section, under Remedy.

R
Review

What's Next

In Step 4, you'll learn how to:

- Best respond to workplace dysfunction based on the results of your Review, including holding people accountable, communicating clear expectations, and supporting individuals in making necessary changes to their workplace behavior, performance or communication

R
Review

STEP 4 — REMEDY AND PROBLEM SOLVING

In Step 3, you conducted an objective Review. Based on that Review, you should now have answers to the following questions:

- What happened (in relation to each alleged concern/incident)?
- Was anything about what happened a violation of workplace policies or procedures or objectively offensive or dysfunctional?
- If so, who caused or contributed to the dysfunction uncovered in your Review?

Now, in Step 4, Remedy and Problem Solving, you'll use your answers to these questions to design a specific a remedial plan for each person found to have contributed to the workplace dysfunction at issue.

The role of a remedial plan is to advise individuals of their specific role in and responsibility for the workplace dysfunction, outline your expectations of them moving forward, and assist them in meeting those expectations. Most problems are solved by clearly letting people know where they went wrong and how to make it right.

R
Remedy

Any Remedy, from the most basic to complex should include two components:

- **Accountability:** Using non-disciplinary or disciplinary measures, let individuals know that specific past communication, behavior or performance is unacceptable or dysfunctional and needs to change
- **Support:** Provide individuals with training, counselling and other interventions to help them make the necessary changes

Determining the Level of Accountability

An individual's level of accountability is determined according to:

- The seriousness of his or her workplace dysfunction established in your Review, based on the **frequency** or amount of dysfunction (in other words, how many allegations were confirmed and how often did each happen) and the **severity** of dysfunction (in other words, how serious was the person's dysfunctional behavior, communication or performance)

Remedy

Outcome of Review

Findings from the Objective Review:

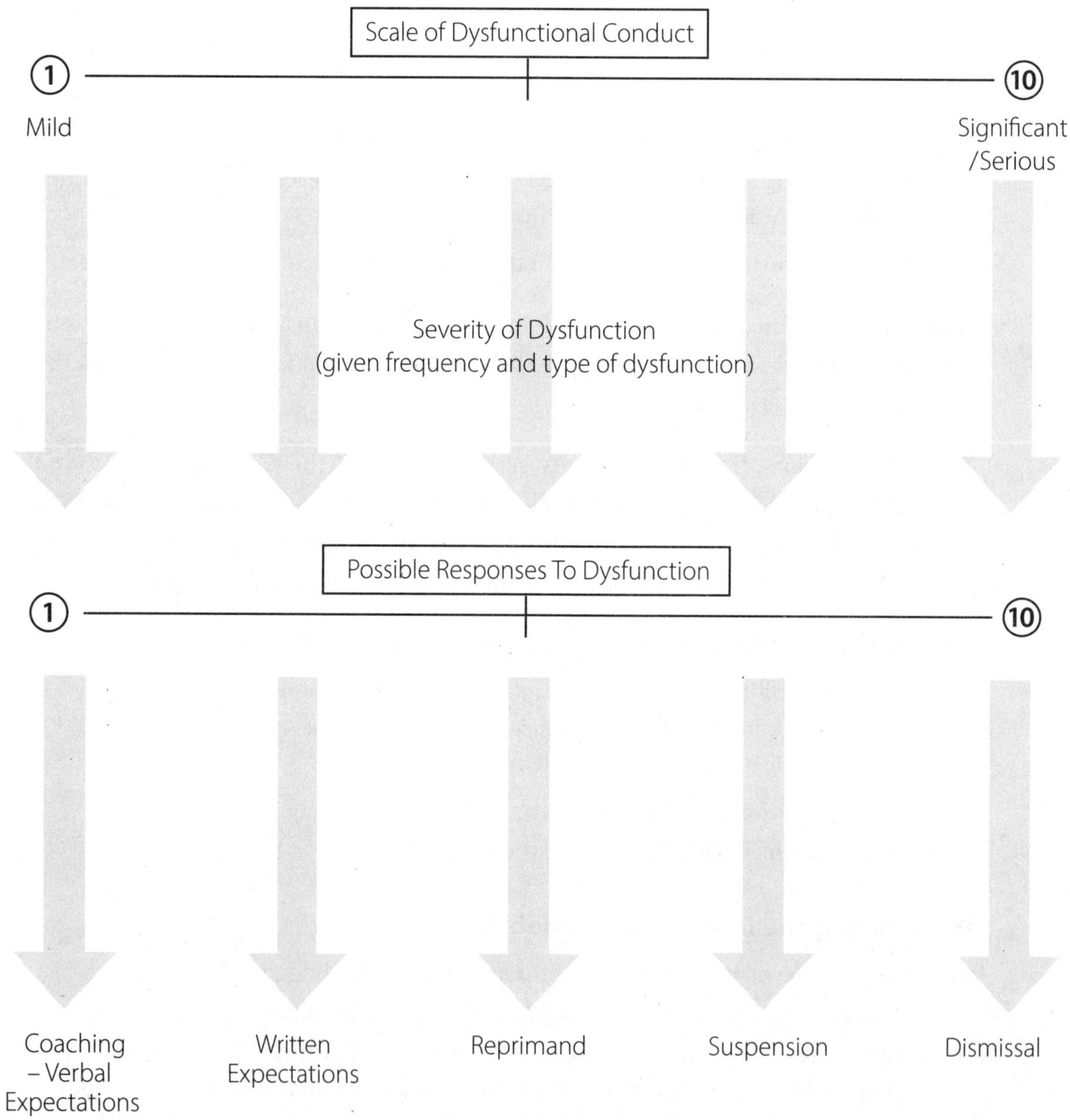

Figure 12: Remedy

R
Remedy

- Whether or not the individual has been previously held accountable for workplace dysfunction (such as prior coaching, letters, or formal discipline)

In Step 2, we introduced you to a Scale of Dysfunctional Conduct to use when Triaging complaints (see Figure 6).

In this section, a similar scale shown in Figure 12, Remedy, will help you determine your response to dysfunction based upon the outcome of your Review. This tool is most applicable in circumstances where the individual under Review does not have an active performance management plan or prior disciplinary record.

Figure 12 shows you how to determine your response to specific findings from your Review. If your findings and conclusions confirmed only one or two mild issues of concern, then your response should fall at the minor end of the scale – and might warrant a coaching conversation.

If the incidents happened with greater frequency or were more serious, then you might start with a Letter of Expectations.

If the frequency or severity of issues were moderately to significantly serious, then you need to impose a formal disciplinary response.

In addition to this general framework, you need to obtain and consider specific organizational policies, and collective agreements that might speak to the level of accountability warranted in certain situations.

It's not sufficient to determine your response based solely on the findings and conclusions of your Review. You also must consider the individual's history of behavior and performance within your organization and whether he or she has been held accountable previously.

Figure 13, The Stove of Accountability, assists you with this step. It shows you how to determine your response to an individual who is already operating under a performance management or progressive disciplinary plan.

Stove of Accountability

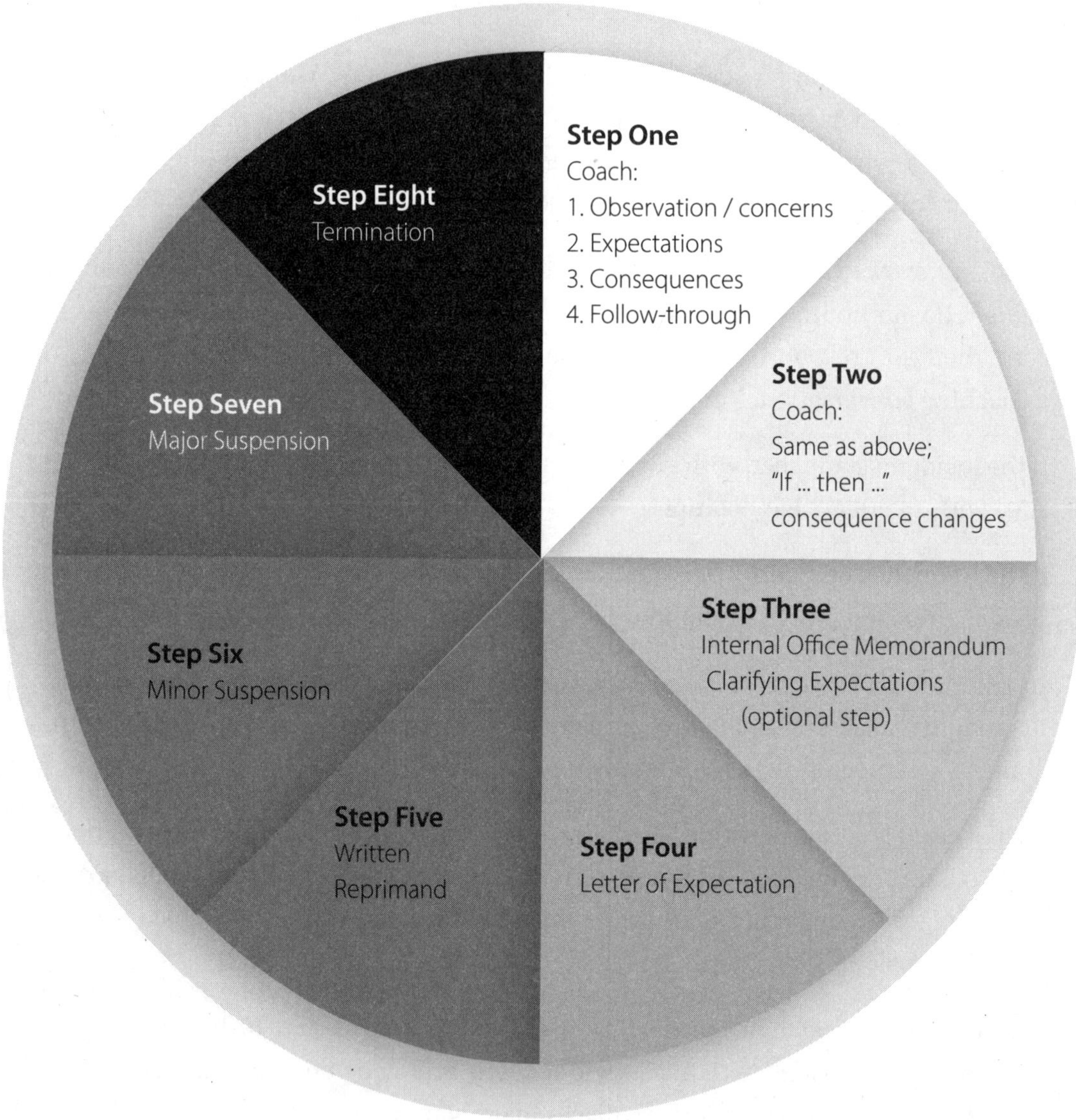

Figure 13: Stove of Accountability

R
Remedy

As you can see from Figure 13, the Stove of Accountability begins with non-disciplinary measures, such as coaching and escalates to formal discipline. The final step is termination of employment.

If the individual under Review is already on the "Stove" because of past infractions, then you need to escalate your response to the next level on the Stove even if your findings from your Review might have warranted something less.

As with every step of the MIRROR Method, it is important to share the outcome of your Review as well your proposed remedial plan with your HR department and, in certain situations, with your in-house or external legal counsel to ensure your proposed Remedy is considered defensible in all the circumstances.

Non-Disciplinary Accountability

The role of accountability is to ensure individuals are clearly advised of and held responsible for their role in any workplace dysfunction. Accountability is not restricted to formal discipline. It does, however, require clear communication of past inappropriate behavior, performance or communication.

If your Review establishes that an individual's unacceptable behavior or performance is mild or infrequent, **and** the individual has not been held accountable for any past workplace dysfunction, then you should begin with non-disciplinary measures.

Such measures include coaching conversations (the MIRROR Discussion), memoranda to file and letters of expectation.

Coaching Conversations: the MIRROR Discussion

Individuals are often unaware of how they show up at work and impact those around them. Their lack of self-awareness (as opposed to intentional malice), plays a significant role in the dysfunction that results in the complaints against them.

Employees have a responsibility to change their unacceptable behavior and meet your expectations, intentional or not. However, they cannot and should not be expected to change their behavior by having to read your mind or the minds of others.

A first step in holding individuals accountable is to let them know of your concerns and expectations through a coaching conversation using the MIRROR Discussion. Remember, the individuals you speak with don't have to agree with your findings, concerns or expectations. They simply need to be made aware of them.

In a MIRROR Discussion, make sure you:

- Communicate your findings, conclusions and concerns flowing from the Review (however informal that Review may have been).
- Reflect for the individual, in a respectful manner and with a measured tone, how they are showing up at work, how they are impacting others, and how they are contributing to current workplace dysfunction. Base your reflections on specific examples from the findings from your Review. Offering vague feedback ("you were disrespectful with that customer") or broad and permanent-sounding generalizations ("you are unprofessional") is counterproductive.
- Do not argue or debate your findings and conclusions with the employee. The opportunity for input arose during your initial meeting with the employee (that is, during the Review itself), and should not be re-visited when communicating the outcome.
- Ensure the individual can picture what it is about their behavior or performance that was found to have been unacceptable.
- Use non-inflammatory language and respectful non-verbal behavior throughout the discussion.
- Set out your expectations for the individual's future performance and behavior at the workplace. It is not enough to tell individuals what they are doing wrong. It is equally important to tell them how to make it right.
- At the end of the discussion, ask individuals how you can support them in meeting these expectations. These supports would be in addition to any you already have determined to be necessary.
- Advise individuals that you will be reviewing the situation on a regular basis and will need to take further action if you do not see sufficient improvement.

Written Memos to File or Letters of Expectation

If the individual had been coached for workplace dysfunction prior to your Review, or if the findings and conclusions from your Review warrant more than a coaching conversation (but less than discipline), you can issue a non-disciplinary Memo to File or Letter of Expectations. Both are similar, except the Letter of Expectations has a more formal appearance and feel to it (as it is often placed on corporate letterhead).

These written documents are like coaching conversations in that their purpose is to let individuals know of your expectations based on the results of your Review. They are not meant to reprimand individuals about specific past incidents (this would be a written reprimand). They are intended to offer a clear description of how individuals need to behave or perform in the future to properly contribute to a functional workplace.

In these circumstances, it is often helpful to have a MIRROR Discussion with the individual and then immediately follow up with a Memo to File or Letter of Expectations confirming that discussion. The letter should clearly reiterate your expectations. Again, it is important to use respectful language and a measured tone, both during the initial meeting and in the follow up correspondence.

Formal Discipline Accountability

If the findings of your Review indicate that the behavioral or performance concerns are sufficiently frequent or serious (in that they fall within 5 to 10 on the Scale of Dysfunctional Conduct), **or** you confirm that the individual has already been issued a Letter of Expectations or more, you likely need to impose formal discipline.

As reflected in both Figure 12 and Figure 13, formal discipline may include: written reprimands, disciplinary suspensions (paid/unpaid), and dismissals. Again, the specific disciplinary measures available at your workplace depend on the employment status of the individual and the specific contracts, agreements, policies, procedures and laws in force at the time.

The Role of Extenuating Circumstances

In Step 3, Conducting a Review, you learned that individuals often try to explain away inappropriate or unacceptable behavior. Some of these reasons are set out in Figure 14, The Why Does Not Justify the How.

The many reasons for unacceptable behavior do not immunize individuals from the consequences of that behavior. People need to be held accountable for their actions regardless of the circumstances or factors that have contributed to their situation.

At times, extenuating circumstances may reduce the severity of the measure or penalty imposed. For example, if someone lost her temper immediately after hearing tragic news about a family member, the level of accountability typically associated with that behavior might be reduced given the circumstances. However, the tragic news itself should not create complete immunity from any consequences for this unacceptable workplace behavior.

For this reason, it's important to share with HR and legal counsel any explanations or excuses you heard during your Review. This will help ensure that the accountability imposed on the individual is defensible given all of the circumstances at play.

The WHY Does Not Justify the How

But it is Important to Understand the WHY to Solve the Problem

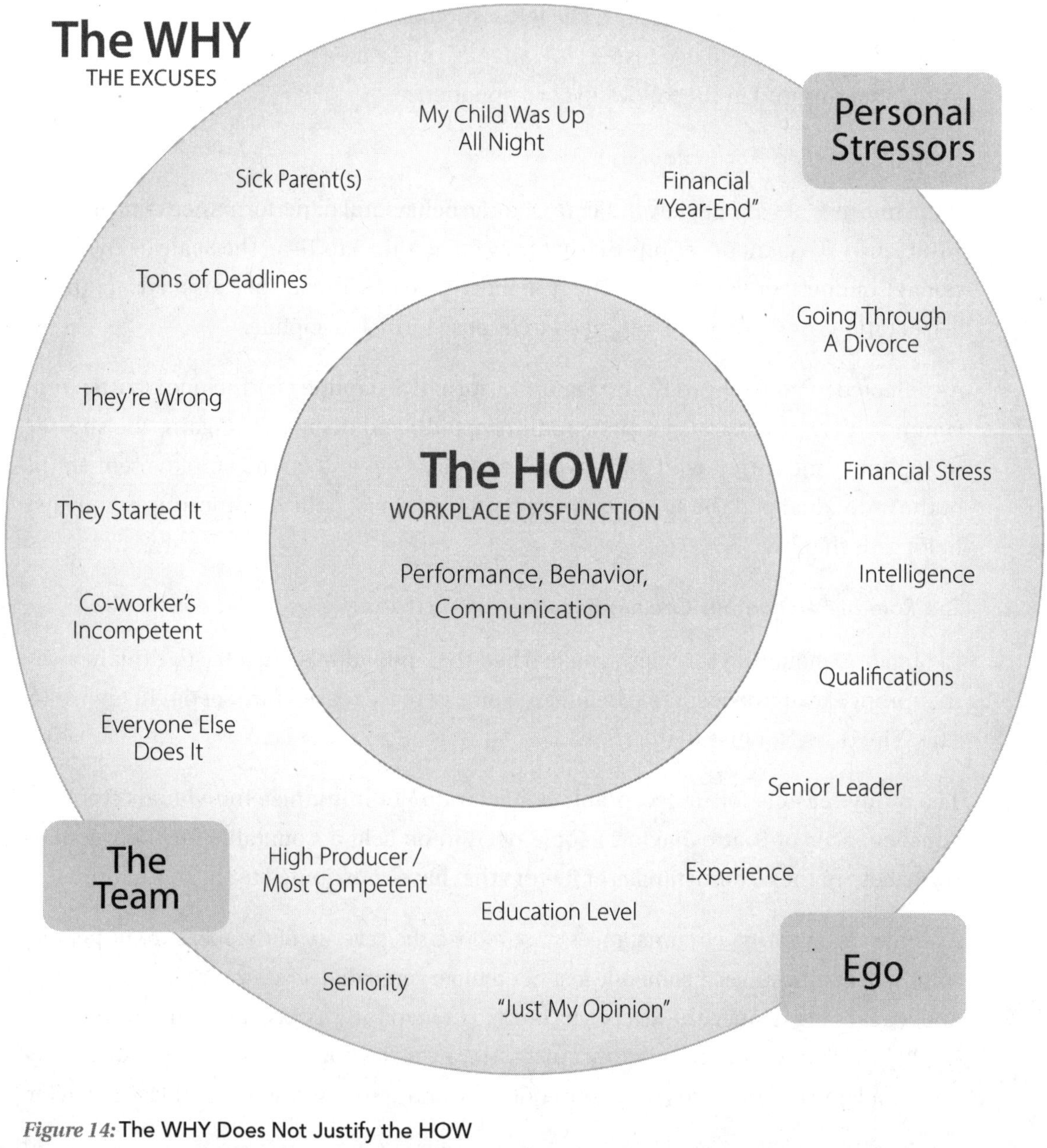

Figure 14: **The WHY Does Not Justify the HOW**

Determining Supports

After determining the appropriate level of accountability, you need to decide what type of supports to implement to assist the employee in moving forward. Supports help individuals make necessary changes to their behavior to meet your expectations.

Remember, this is *in addition to*, not *in place of*, accountability.

This is another reason to carefully consider an individual's WHYs for their behavior, that is, their explanations for why they did what they did. For example, if an individual's explanation for being rude to a customer is family stress, then one support you might offer is counselling through a confidential employee assistance program.

If the excuse for making errors is the new software program, then you might arrange additional training or the assignment of an internal coach for further mentoring and direction.

At a more serious level, if someone attributes significant misconduct to a mental health condition or to a drug or alcohol addiction, then your supports might include a medical leave of absence to allow them to attend treatment, and perhaps specific workplace accommodations to address any residual medical limitations.

The MIRROR Method book outlines numerous examples of supports to consider. The specific ones you select in any given case should be based upon the information you obtained during and after your Review, and the nature of supports available both within your organization and through your related insurance plans and benefit coverage.

Some supports may be imposed by you (and are mandatory in nature), and some may be based on reasonable requests made by the employee.

When you meet with individuals to share the findings and conclusions of your Review, you also need to advise them of the remedial plan you have devised in response. This should include the level of accountability being imposed, your expectations of them in the future, and any supports that you will be implementing to assist them in meeting your expectations.

You need to follow this process for each individual found to have been involved in any and all workplace dysfunction uncovered by your Review.

CASE STUDY: DESIGNING REMEDIAL PLANS FOR MIKE AND JOE

Following your Review of Mike's comment to Joe, assume that you've made the following findings and conclusions:

- Prefer Joe's version of events
- Determine that Mike made the comment to Joe in a sarcastic manner
- Conclude that the comment is objectively viewed as unreasonable and disrespectful
- Determine that this was not the first time that Mike had been blatantly sarcastic or dismissive at work
- Determine that despite this history, Mike has not been held accountable for his past workplace dysfunction
- Accept as credible Mike's explanation for making this statement (Mike was going through personal issues at the time)

In view of these findings and conclusions, your remedial plan for Mike might be as follows:

- **Accountability:** This type of dysfunction falls on the mild end of the Scale of Dysfunctional Conduct, standing alone and given the lack of accountability imposed in the past. For this reason, you likely would have a coaching conversation with Mike and possibly issue him a Memorandum to File, in which you set out your expectations for respectful communication in the workplace.
- **Support:** Mike's personal issues will not immunize him from accountability for his disrespectful behavior at work. However, you should respond to these issues – not only because it's the right thing to do, but also to assist Mike in meeting your expectations for change. Your supports for Mike might include:
  - Referral to a Family Assistance Program or individual counselling to learn about coping strategies if his personal situation appears to be ongoing
  - Basic contact information about the Family Assistance Program if the situation has passed so he has this information for future reference
  - Written materials on respectful workplace communication

R
Remedy

If you also determine that Joe contributed to workplace dysfunction by being unreasonably resistant to feedback or not open to variations in work practices, then you need to develop a remedial plan for him as well. Remember, Joe's resistance does not justify Mike's sarcastic response to him but at the same time, it needs to be addressed independent from any action you take with Mike. You need to Remedy *every* aspect of workplace dysfunction confirmed through your Review rather than respond to one individual's dysfunctional behavior to the exclusion of others.

Accountability for Joe might warrant a MIRROR Discussion with him which includes specifics on:

- How he is showing up for others
- How his approach may be getting in the way of his own success
- How respectful communication includes tolerance for different ideas, opinions and work practices

This might need to involve more than a MIRROR Discussion if you have addressed these concerns with Joe in the past.

Your supports might include: one-on-one formal mentoring with a senior coworker within or outside his team; additional training on regulatory practices specific to this workplace; additional scheduled check-ins with his supervisor or manager; and any other reasonable suggestions that Joe might suggest.

Again, the specifics of your supports will be based on the findings of your Review and feedback from Joe.

R
Remedy

What's Next

In Step 5, you'll learn how to:

- Help organizations restore trust, communication and respect between individuals or amongst teams

STEP 5 — OPERATIONAL RESTORATION (OR REMEDYING TEAM DYSFUNCTION)

In Step 4, you designed remedial plans for individuals on your team. Step 5, Operational Restoration, is about helping to restore communication, stability and trust between individuals or amongst the team as a whole.

Operational restoration might be necessary because of many different circumstances including:

- Specific events, conflicts or circumstances that led to the Review
- Longstanding conflict between two or more individuals that came to light during the Review
- Longstanding team dynamics that came to light during the Review
- Team tension, cliques, or camps that may have arisen as a result of the Review

Operational Restoration offers individuals and teams a safe and confidential process in which to *debrief* past experiences (such as perceived betrayals, misunderstandings, and disrespectful behavior) and a*gree* on ways to move forward and work together in a respectful and productive manner.

What is the Most Appropriate Restorative Process?

Figure 15, Operational Restoration for Teams, highlights a few different types of Operational Restoration to consider, depending on the specific circumstances and team dynamics at play.

If your Review focused on the dysfunctional behavior or performance of one individual who had minimal impact on the broader team dynamics, then you likely don't need to engage in any processes beyond the remedial plan you created for that individual.

However, if you identified dysfunction by one person that had a direct and lasting impact on another person, or you noticed a dysfunctional relationship *between* two individuals, then you might want to arrange a mediation for those involved. This is not the same as a facilitated discussion or mediation that takes place as an informal Review. This is a mediation that happens after any Review—formal or informal—and is done in addition to individual remedial plans to clear the air and improve future working relationships.

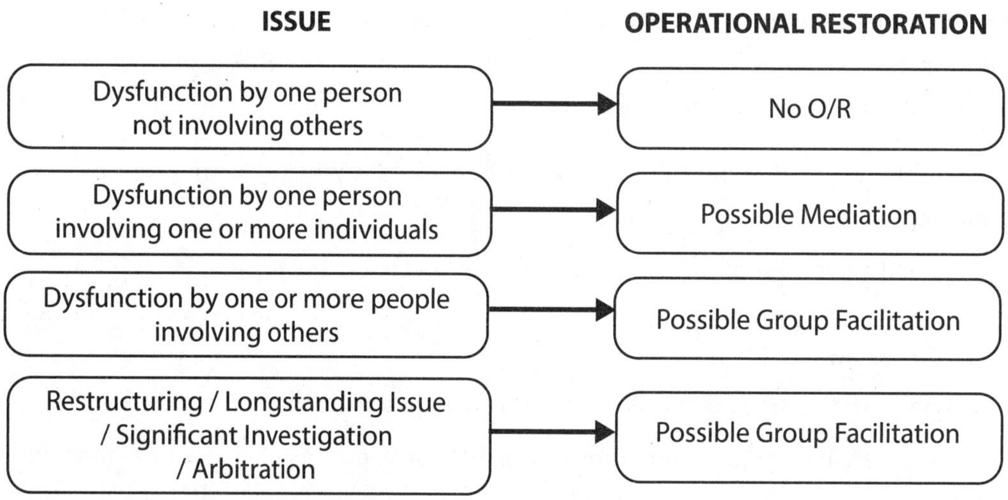

Figure 15: Operational Restoration for Teams

If longstanding or systemic concerns are identified, or the Review itself has created or aggravated team-wide tensions, then the entire team should engage in a structured team rebuilding process. This is a critical first step in rebuilding trust in a fractured team. Through this process, teams use their past experiences to develop mutually agreeable rules of engagement or principles of communication. These help guide them in future interactions.

You or another leader may be able to facilitate mediations between two or three individuals if you have the perceived neutrality, training and confidence to do so. Otherwise, it is best to have a third party, outside your team, facilitate this process.

Operational Restoration that involves the entire team should be facilitated by someone outside your department, preferably someone external to your organization. This person should have extensive experience in team *rebuilding* in the context of significant workplace change, restructuring or high conflict situations. This is a unique skill set and one that differs markedly from general team building.

The Importance of Closure

Following any mediation or broader restorative process, individuals should be expected to let go of the past and move forward in a constructive manner, at least while they are at work. Workplace discussions or criticism about what happened should end.

Individuals who behave or communicate in a manner that is resistant to the principles and agreements reached through Operational Restoration should be held accountable by following the steps of the MIRROR Method.

CASE STUDY: HELPING JOE'S TEAM

Based on the findings and conclusions in the case study, possible Operational Restoration could include the following:

- Mediation between Joe and Mike
- Mediation between Laurie and Joe
- Team facilitation/staff meeting about workplace respect, communication, social media, orientation of new employees, conflict resolution and other matters highlighted during the Review

What's Next

In Step 6, you'll learn how to:

- Follow up with individuals and teams to make sure the workplace is back on track

O
Operational Restoration

STEP 6 — REVISITING THE SCENE OF THE DYSFUNCTION

The final step in the MIRROR Method requires you to Revisit individual remedial plans as well as any agreements reached through Operational Restoration to determine if these interventions have successfully remedied the workplace dynamics.

This should be done within three months of the processes being completed (or sooner if new issues are reported or observed).

Individual Remedial Plans

In Revisiting individual remedial plans, you should:

- Ensure that mandated courses, training and mentoring have been completed and any other workplace supports and accommodations have been properly implemented
- Determine if there are continuing or new concerns with an individual's behavior, communication or performance despite implementation of the remedial plan

If Remedial Plans Have Not Been Fully Implemented

If the supports have not been implemented successfully, then you need to determine why. If this is the result of a housekeeping error, such as administrative oversight on the part of the employer or individual, then you need to fix this as soon as possible. If it is due to the employee refusing or resisting such supports, such as failing to attend a scheduled training course, then you need to Review and address this resistance using the MIRROR Method.

Team Check-ins

In Revisiting agreements reached through Operational Restoration (such as rules of engagement or guidelines of communication), you should check in with your team on a regular and ongoing basis to determine whether systemic issues have been resolved (or are improving). It might be that the agreements originally reached by the team need to be tweaked or updated. It might be that the agreements work well but one or two members of the team appear to be interacting in a manner inconsistent with them.

No one is expected to like or agree with a remedial plan or restorative process. They must, however, respect and comply with any outcomes of the MIRROR Method, including expectations of their supervisor or agreements reached through rules of engagement, team charters or otherwise. Any apparent refusal to do so should be Reviewed and addressed using the MIRROR Method.

Every time your Review confirms inappropriate behavior or performance on the part of the same individuals, you need to ensure that you escalate accountability in your remedial plan, using the Stove of Accountability, and reconsider the effectiveness of the supports you have implemented.

CASE STUDY: REVISITING JOE'S TEAM

In Revisiting the issues at Joe's worksite, you will need to check on any concerns that were identified in the Review and addressed in the remedial plans and restorative processes. This might include:

- Checking in with Joe for an update on his experiences at work and Mike's treatment of him
- Checking in with Laurie and possibly others to determine how Mike and Joe are doing
- Meeting with Joe's mentor to ensure that mentoring is in progress or completed and learning about the mentor's views on the process
- Ensuring that Joe has completed any mandated training on regulatory practices
- Checking in with Mike to confirm that he has attended any mandated counselling or courses on respectful communication
- Checking in with the team to see if there are any residual or new concerns about workplace respect, communication, regulatory compliance or otherwise

If you identify ongoing concerns, then you need to engage the MIRROR Method once again to diagnose the issues and devise customized and updated remedial plans or restorative processes based on your most recent Review.

What's Next? Review, Remedy and Revisit

Congratulations! You've made it to the end of the MIRROR Method process.

Changing human behavior is a process of trial and error. If you realize that your remedial plans and restorative processes have not been successful, don't panic! Simply re-engage the MIRROR Method and try again to correct any dysfunctional behavior or performance.

If you diligently continue this process of "Review, Remedy and Revisit", you will ultimately achieve one of two outcomes: individuals will either change their behavior and performance to meet your expectations, or they will no longer be a part of your team.

While the latter option is not the desired outcome, it may be necessary if individuals continue to engage in dysfunctional behavior or unacceptable performance despite numerous attempts to facilitate change.

What you need to know is that—with either option—you have done all you can to build a respectful and productive environment for your team and organization overall.

That's the magic of the MIRROR Method.

R

Revisit

Timeline of Events

Employee Name:

Date	Event (meeting, communication with employee, cancellations, coaching)	Follow-up / Action Completed

Team Snapshot Form

A. General Baseline of Individual Performance

1. **Name of Employee** (Senior Leaders to include Managers and Supervisors in this Assessment)

[ ]

2. **Any past reported or observed concerns re Individual Job Performance?** Circle all that might apply:

   Productivity   Accuracy   Safe Practices   Documentation

   Customer Service (incl. public, patients, students, family, clients)   Other (specify) ____________________

3. **Any past reported or observed concerns re Reliability as a Team Player?** Circle all that might apply:

   Attendance   Punctuality   Trustworthiness   Assisting Coworkers

   Information Sharing & General Transparency   Respect for Supervisory Authority & Direction

   Respectful Workplace Communication (gossip, verbal and/or non-verbal disrespect)

   Tolerance & Respect for Diversity (in work preferences and individual background)

   Other (specify) ____________________

4. **If YES:**

   Has employee been made aware of these issues/concerns? Yes / No (circle one)

   Is employee on a formal performance improvement plan/progressive disciplinary track? Yes / No (circle one)

B. General Baseline of Team Performance

1. **Any observations or available metrics regarding the rate of turnover (including resignations and internal transfers), in general and as compared to other departments?**

[ ]

2. **Any observations or available metrics regarding the rate of sick leave (including Workers Compensation and disability leaves) in general and as compared to other departments?**

[ ]

Real-time Complaint Form

The Duty to Inquire

1. Name of Employee(s) / Team with Potential Issue

2. **Nature of Concern?** Circle all that might apply:

   a. **Any past reported or observed concerns re Individual Job Performance?**

   Productivity   Accuracy   Safe Practices   Documentation

   Customer Service (incl. public, patients, students, family, clients)   Other (specify) ____________________

   b. **Any past reported or observed concerns re Reliability as a Team Player?**

   Attendance   Punctuality   Trustworthiness   Assisting Coworkers

   Information Sharing & General Transparency   Respect for Supervisory Authority & Direction

   Respectful Workplace Communication (gossip, verbal and/or non-verbal disrespect)

   Tolerance & Respect for Diversity (in work preferences and individual background)

   Other (specify) ____________________

3. **Source of Concern?** Circle all that might apply:

   Reported to Leader   Observed by Workplace Leader   Other (specify) ____________________

4. **If Reported to a Leader:**

   a. **Who reported complaint?**

   Name:

   Relationship to Organization: Circle one

   Employee   Leader   Other (specify) ____________________
   (e.g. Customer, Supplier, Member of Public, etc.)

   Contact Information:

Form cont'd: "Real-Time" Complaint or Concern: the Duty to Inquire

4. cont'd:

   b. **Outline what was reported:** Fill in below and/or attach a copy of the text/email

   c. **Outline any background that is potentially relevant to the concern (e.g. prior concerns, prior history):** Fill in below and/or attach additional notes

   d. **Outline any direct steps taken by individual before reporting the concern and the response by the subject employee (including his/her demeanor to the feedback):** Fill in below and/or attach additional notes

Form cont'd: "Real-Time" Complaint or Concern: the Duty to Inquire

5. If directly observed by the workplace leader:

   a. Outline what was specifically witnessed including what was heard and why it was of concern (if not readily apparent to a layperson). Include a description of behaviors, not a label, judgment or characterization of those behaviors (e.g. state that "he/she was speaking with a loud voice with a red face and a stern expression" NOT "he was speaking inappropriately or aggressively or angrily"): Fill in below and/or attach additional notes

   b. Outline any relevant background in relation to this situation (relevant history of the individuals involved, prior expectations to the subject employee, similar past complaints): Fill in below and/or attach additional notes

   c. Outline any immediate discussions or other steps taken in response to the observed concern:
   Fill in below and/or attach additional notes

   NONE yet, or:

Checklist A: Setting up the Review

Factors to Consider

Factors To Consider	✓	**Date(s)** (if applicable)
Have the necessary parties/individuals been informed of the review?		
Has each individual been cautioned about confidentiality and retaliation?		
Have interim measures (transfers/suspensions of certain individuals/adjustment of reporting structure) been considered and if necessary implemented?		
Has the appropriate investigator (experienced, neutral) been retained?		
Has the investigator been given instructions on scope and timing of investigation?		
Has the appropriate venue been considered and selected (on/off-site)?		
Has requested or mandated representation been arranged?		
Have all other relevant procedural requirements in specific collective agreements, workplace policies and contracts been met?		

Checklist B: Conducting the Review

Conducting the Interview - General Principles	✓	**Date(s)** (if applicable)
Each individual has been told (again) about confidentiality and non-retaliation		
Each witness has been advised of the importance of being open and honest		
All particulars (who, what, when, where) about each reported "concern"/event are canvassed with all relevant individuals (witnesses and parties)		
Questions are **open-ended** and **open-minded**		
All labels are 'broken down' into specific behaviors, actions or statements (e.g. what did the person mean by "unsafe" – what behaviors/communication did they see as unsafe? Or, what did they mean by aggressive or intimidating? What were the demonstrable behaviors or statements of concern?)		
Any and all potentially relevant documents are obtained and reviewed (e.g. emails, letters, available Facebook posts, texts, timecards, expense reports, logs, receipts, complaint forms, manager's notes, etc.)		
Disrespectful or other notable behavior during the interview is documented and if necessary, addressed at the time		
After interviewing complainant and his/her witnesses, interview the accused		
If the responses from the accused differ from those you obtained during the course of the investigation, put the information/discrepancy to the accused and ask for a response		
Do not "hide" anything from the accused. Give him/her an opportunity to consider the particulars of the concerns against him/her as well as time to respond and explain his/her perspective		
Interview witnesses relevant to the accused's version of events		
Re-interview specific individuals, if necessary, to effectively consider evidence/explanations from accused		
Complete a process timeline throughout the investigation (e.g. steps taken, date/time/name of the individual interviewed, documents requested/obtained/reviewed)		
Take and date neutral, factual notes of interviews		

Checklist B cont'd: Conducting the Review

Conducting the Interview	✓	**Date(s)** (if applicable)
Include non-verbal behaviors in interview in the notes (e.g. long pauses, sighing, laughing sarcastically, remorse, crying, anger etc.).		
Prepare Summaries of Evidence based on Interview notes		
Make Findings of fact based on the assessment of all of the evidence and credibility of those interviewed		
Draw conclusions as to whether any relevant legislation/policy/procedure has been breached (based on the Findings of Fact)		
If part of the mandate, develop recommendations		

Checklist C: Review Questions

Sample Questions to Consider Not Exhaustive - Please Customize	✓
What happened?	
Describe what it looked like to you?	
When did it/they happen?	
Who was present?	
Who did or said what (including you)?	
In what order?	
Is there any notes/documents?	
Who else may have relevant information? Explain	
What happened afterwards?	
Who did you speak with? What did you say?	
Why was there a delay in reporting the incident(s)/concern(s) (if applicable)? Explain	
What has been the impact on the person at work?	
Is there anything else you think I should know?	
Is there anything that you think is important that I may have missed?	

If there is more than one allegation/incident, ask the questions set out above again.

Possible Additional Questions for the Accused Fill in below and/or attach additional notes/questions	✓